Endorsements

There is a sad dearth of books advocating biblical eldership that also address the crucial issues involved in improving elder leadership and effectiveness. Not a theoretician but a practitioner of the truths he presents, Dick Swartley has spent a lifetime thinking about the issues of biblical church government, and has been at the forefront of establishing a biblically ordered church that has a worldwide outreach. He exposes the distortions of eldership and sets forth a positive practical vision for effective church eldership.

This book is particularly helpful for growing churches, with excellent insights and suggestions for enhancing prayer, elders-staff relations, planning, consensus building, decision making, and communication with the congregation. I highly recommend this valuable work as standard reading for church leaders. It fills a big gap.

Alexander Strauch
Author of *Biblical Eldership*
Elder, Littleton Bible Chapel, Littleton, Colorado

While there are good books on the theology of eldership, Dick Swartley's work carefully addresses the practice of eldership. It is clarifying, challenging, and convincing, and I commend its common sense linking of solid biblical insight with the real-life struggles those of us in church leadership all share.

Doug Goins
Former Pastor Elder; now Pastor-At-Large and Missionary,
Peninsula Bible Church, Palo Alto, California

For me, the philosophy of ministry of the church is an area of expertise and a real-time, hot-button issue. Clad in my scholar's hat and my churchman's experience, I am very picky (sometimes downright ornery) when I encounter others' attempts to give insight and direction on the biblical functioning of the church. Usually, I walk away from such books with great disappointment, saddened anew that another author just did not get it. But, I can say unashamedly that Dick Swartley gets it in this book!

I have not read any other book on church leadership and governing that so fully integrates the biblical and wisely, practical! Dick draws from his graduate theological training and over forty years' experience of providing the kind of leadership of which he speaks. The work is the author's mature expression of biblical interpretation and decades of wise leading in the church. I recommend that it be put in the hands of as many elders, pastors, seminary professors, and students as possible. This fantastic book will be immensely helpful to those who will have to give an account to Jesus Christ for their leadership role in His Church.

Walt Russell, Ph.D.
Author of *Playing with Fire*
Professor of New Testament, Talbot School of Theology
Biola University, Los Angeles; Church Consultant

Eldership in Action

Through
BIBLICAL
GOVERNANCE
of the CHURCH

Richard H. Swartley

ECS
M I N I S T R I E S
The Word to the World

EMMAUS COLLEGE PRESS

Eldership in Action: Through Biblical Governance of the Church
Richard H. Swartley

Copyright © 2005 ECS Ministries

Published by:
ECS Ministries
P.O. Box 1028
Dubuque, IA   52004-1028
www.ecsministries.org

Library of Congress Cataloging in Publication Data

Swartley, Richard H., 1934–
    Eldership in action: through biblical governance of the church /
Richard H. Swartley
    Includes bibliographical references and indexes.
    ISBN 1-59387-016-7
    1. Church governance. 2. Elders 3. Church officers I. Title.

Printed in the United States of America

Contents

Acknowledgments 7
Preface 8

1. **Biblical Eldership** 11
    The Problem 11
    Biblical Eldership 13
    Distinction in Function, Not Different Offices 14
    An Invalid Distinction 16
    Plurality and Leadership 19

2. **Biblical Governance** 22
    The Challenge 24
    New Testament Perspective on Leadership 25
    Distortions of the Biblical Model 38
    Can the New Testament Model Work Today? 42
    What Is the Real Impediment? 47

3. **The Elder** 49
    Appointment of Elders 49
    Term Limits 63
    Relationships 66
    Prerequisites for Governing Biblically 73

4. **The Elder Council** 76
    Responsibilities of the Council 76
    Size of the Elder Council 80
    Delegation 85
    Relating to and Recruiting Staff 93
    Relationship with the Congregation 96

5.   Planning   100
Terminology   102
Shared Values   106
Vision Statement   107
Mission Statement   111
SWOT Analysis   112
Strategies   115
Goals   116
Objectives   117
Tactics   118
Reporting and Accountability   121
The Planning Cycle   121
An Important Caution   121

6.   Council Decisions   123
Making Decisions   124
Threats to Deciding by Consensus   129
Functional Barriers to Leading by Consensus   136
The Role of the Moderator   140
Handling the Major Decisions   142
Involving the Congregation   154
Confidentiality   158
Emergency Decisions   160

7.   Efficient Council Meetings   162
Communication   163
The Agenda and Supporting Documents   164
Virtual Meetings   166
Prayer   167
Ministry Reports   167
Minutes   168
Policy Manual   169
The Challenge   170

Conclusion   171
Notes   173
Bibliography   177
Scripture Index   181
General Index   183
About the Author   189

Acknowledgments

O F IMMEASURABLE ASSISTANCE AND ENCOURAGEMENT in the preparation of this work were those who also labor to promote biblical leadership of Christ's church. Ben Able, Paul Apple, Tom Arnsberg, John Ellis, Doug Goins, Dr. Vern Mittelstadt, Dr. Walt Russell, Alexander Strauch, and Paul Winslow not only supported the value of the project with enthusiasm, but graciously reviewed the manuscript at various stages of completion. These brothers' sound advice and helpful suggestions have made a significant contribution. Their insights have been especially valuable, since each has had substantial, but different, experience in church leadership and in working out the implications of the New Testament teaching on church governance. I am especially grateful for their candor in disagreeing with me over various issues. These cautions have prompted reexamination of many questions, leading to a better overall result.

I also thank my wife, Anne, for her help in all aspects of this project. Because of her mastery of the subject and knowledge of Scripture, her contributions have been invaluable. This work demonstrates the effects of her loving encouragement and probing questions.

Preface

IN 1986, **ALEXANDER STRAUCH** authored *Biblical Eldership, An Urgent Call to Restore Biblical Eldership.*[1] This definitive work has sold more than 145 thousand copies in English, and in translations used around the world. The effect on the thinking of the leadership of the church has been profound, and, consequently, many are evaluating the governance and leadership styles of their churches.

I have enjoyed the privilege of working with Alexander Strauch in producing companions to his work, *The Study Guide to Biblical Eldership* and *The Mentor's Guide to Biblical Eldership.*[2] As the result of this association, I have spoken with many church leaders who are now convinced of the biblical imperative that our churches be elder-led. But these men struggle with issues of implementation. They are especially frustrated with the overt (or covert) conflicts they encounter when attempting to institute biblical governance. These challenges manifest themselves as:

- Cultural resistance to biblical eldership in churches attempting change.

- Failure of churches to grow sufficiently to meet community needs, despite their being faithful to the biblical directives. Or, alternatively,

- Loss of their biblical character by churches as they experience growth.

However, many have also described enthusiastically how the concept of biblical eldership has been life-changing! They speak of how pastors, elders, and whole elder councils have been prompted to study the entire issue and reconsider their own roles in the church's

PREFACE

governance. Though transformed and encouraged as they enter these new waters, it is not surprising that they face many questions.

It has been exactly in empathetic response that I have reached out to partner with these brothers—in church plants and in churches experiencing growing pains. For some time, they have encouraged me to explain in detail how a church can be truly biblical in its governance and leadership, while simultaneously accomplishing the Great Commission effectively in our day. My focus will be on the elders' collective responsibilities, and the practical aspects of putting biblical structures and methods to work in the church of today. We will explore valid implementations all along the continuum, from the small church, to the church plant, to the large church with many members and ministries. Through an examination of the biblical teaching and explanation of how some outstanding examples function, we will see that the struggle for implementation is well worth the effort.

Although the principles taught throughout this book have broad application to various churches and assemblies, a number relate more specifically to larger evangelical churches with paid staff. While I strive to differentiate between large and small bodies, readers must evaluate the instruction in light of the context in which they serve.

I do not present myself as the expert with all the answers—or as having been associated with a church that is more than a work in progress. Like those of the same mind around the world who are engaged in restoring biblical governance, I am continuing to learn. It has been my privilege and pain to serve as a founding elder in a church (planted in 1972, now with an adult attendance of two thousand), that experienced rapid growth, along the way succumbed twice to its successes, and that, for the most part, has recovered the initial vision of its elders. This recovery has occurred mainly through transitioning from a secular pattern of church leadership to the biblical model for elder leadership.

I am especially grateful to Dr. Walt Russell[3] who redirected the leadership of Church of the Saviour[4] to a biblical model for elder leadership in 1995, during an extensive consultation; and to the staff of the Peninsula Bible Church,[5] for encouragement throughout our transformation, contributed through transparent discussions, backed up by their considerable credibility of more than five decades of biblical governance.

I am also thankful for my own distressing personal failures and the negative experiences God has allowed me. I did not welcome such irritants and taxing of resources. But, having witnessed, both at close hand and from afar, the destructive swath wreaked by unbiblical

PREFACE

leadership in the church, I confess that I have discovered a great deal about the corrupting influence of ego, power, and privilege—as well as men's timidity, passivity, and acquiescence in responsibility. The failed behavior, commission and omission, of our leadership and the resulting turmoil in our churches have driven many of us to repent of past lack of obedience and to reexamine both Scripture's directives on church governance and the biblical parameters of leadership.

For more than thirty years, I have served as a tentmaking elder, while simultaneously employed as an engineer, the last ten years as a senior systems analyst engaged in design and integration of very large government systems. In both venues, I have benefited from a clear picture of the extreme contrast between effective team leadership and injurious autocratic control. In the church, as in government and industry, the inappropriate use of power by a leader may produce short-term gains, but always, over time, at the expense of those he is supposed to be serving.

My heartfelt desire is that all churches maintain, not only high standards of theological purity, but biblical leadership and governance. I pray that this study will aid those who sincerely seek to establish or restore biblical governance of the church, especially those who have already embarked on this venture. For the individual Christian or the community of believers, our maturity in Christ is not only measured by what we know and believe, but by who we are and what we do.

With gratitude to those brothers and sisters who have labored faithfully in the frontline trenches with me, and the prayer that our Lord be glorified,

Dick Swartley
January 2005

I am writing these things to you . . . so that you will know
how one ought to conduct himself in the household of God.
1 Timothy 3:14–15

Chapter 1

Biblical Eldership

WHEN THE FIRST NEW TESTAMENT CHURCHES were being established, Paul sent Titus to Crete to "set in order what remains and appoint elders in every city as I directed you" (Titus 1:5). The apostle was explicit and resolute: The development of the early churches was not to occur haphazardly. Paul was determined that these bodies be structured according to his specific instructions and that they be elder-led. A church is a complex organization. Like other complex organizations, it must be managed well—especially so that its God-given mission may be sustained. The household of God is "the church of the living God, the pillar and support of the truth" (1 Tim. 3:15).

THE PROBLEM

Often these days the governance of the church is intensely frustrating—both for the leadership and for the congregation. From their viewpoint, leaders and pastors complain that their church is stuck in its traditions and culture and, therefore, unable to adapt to the changing environment, or to offer an up-to-date response to the challenge of the Great Commission. Ministry leaders protest that elder boards are unresponsive to their vision, drag their heels, or attempt to micromanage every issue. Entrenched "pillars" of the church struggle with each other and pastors over issues of personal power and influence, instead of seeking Christ's will for the body.

Consider for a moment the outlook, not of those "in charge," but of many in the pew who may not have a clue how their church functions. How its affairs are conducted may be so beyond their field of vision as to be invisible, except for awareness of the usual calls for contributions.

11

Even if the average attendee understands his church government, he generally feels he has no influence on its leadership. (He or she may also be enjoying irresponsible passivity, but that is another matter.) He says that he does not know any leader who cares about his own particular concern, and no elder comes to his ministry with the express purpose of understanding or overseeing it. When the annual congregational meeting rolls around, "Who cares?" These attitudes and objections should give us pause.

Have some of our evangelical churches supposedly retained the mere form of elder leadership, or given it lip service, while, in fact, we have followed other guidelines for so long that we have lost our way? Have the biblical directions for governance by a plurality of elders been abandoned for the sake of expediency? Are we so mired in those methods of governing which were handed down to us from the past that we cannot even imagine implementing biblical guidelines? Or, do we understand the teachings of the New Testament, but believe that implementing them in the church today is impossible?

INADEQUATE SOLUTIONS

In an interview conducted by *Christianity Today,* Larry Osborne shows how far some churches have strayed from the biblical position. Osborne wrote *The Unity Factor*[6] which explores the creation of healthy elder boards. He was asked by the interviewer: "What is the purpose of a board? What should members see as their function?" Osborne replied:

> That [the purpose of an elder board] changes as the church changes. In a smaller church, the purpose is usually helping the pastor get the job done. In a larger church, it's helping a pastor make and communicate good decisions. In the largest churches, a board's primary function is to be the brakes of the organization, the accountability, people who can stop anything. The board is also the wise counsel, because a larger church is staff-led, so the board is more wise counsel than hands-on leaders. They also serve as a crisis team in waiting.[7]

This answer may give an accurate picture of the state of the contemporary church, but it certainly represents clear rejection of Scripture's teaching on the governance of the church. This will become plain as we explore what the New Testament teaches about the role of elders.

Osborne is not alone in his misunderstanding of or departure from biblical instructions on the role of elders. But most just consider the teaching irrelevant and unworkable in the present-day church. This simply need not be the case, because numerous examples exist of churches exemplary in their obedience to the biblical directives for eldership, having healthy, harmonious leaderships and congregations. For many churches, the reexamination of current practices in light of the New Testament design has been the impetus for revival and envisioning of new horizons.

RESULTS OF OBEDIENCE

Responsiveness and relevance to our local culture need not be achieved at the cost of eviscerating the apostles' intent for the governance of the church. From my own experience—and that of leaders in many other churches of all sizes—I am convinced that obedience to the biblical directives results in thriving local churches, bodies that are active in productive evangelism, planting churches, and sending out missionaries. This occurs—*not despite* being faithful to the instructions of the New Testament, but *as the consequence*! Some will object that while biblical eldership works well for the small church, it is impractical for the large church. I disagree and will subsequently show that the New Testament model is applicable to churches of all proportions.

In his definitive *Biblical Eldership*, Alexander Strauch sets forth an accurate, comprehensive, biblical exegesis and interpretation of biblical eldership. He teaches powerfully on the establishment of elder leadership in the early churches, and I strongly recommend this detailed exegesis of the passages defining the apostles' intent. Here, in my work, the biblical argument for elder governance is merely summarized before I advance the main thesis, that *biblical elder direction of the church can be accomplished in our culture and in an effective, practical manner.*

BIBLICAL ELDERSHIP

The New Testament teaches that certain men were collectively endowed with diverse gifts, furnished by the Lord for the founding and maintenance of the early churches (1 Cor. 12:29–30; Eph. 4:11). He provided apostles, prophets, teachers, evangelists, and apostolic delegates like Titus and Timothy. These men participated in the lives of various churches, but none of them ever acted as the permanent head of one congregation. They served multiple churches or labored for a time in a specific place as church planters. The New Testament only mentions two offices, elder and deacon, that were instituted for the management of church affairs. Deacons oversee the collection and distribution of benevolence and do not exercise any governing responsibility. The office of elder is the *sole* position in the church created for the governance of the church. As Strauch, through careful exegesis of Scripture, points out: "Unlike deacons, shepherds [elders] are responsible for the overall leadership, supervision, and teaching of the congregation."[8]

DISTINCTION IN FUNCTION, NOT DIFFERENT OFFICES

But what about the person called "pastor" today? Until we understand who he was in the historical context, we will not have removed a great barrier to understanding the New Testament elder. Clearly, in the early church, the preacher-teacher (in modern usage, the term has become "pastor") did not hold a separate office. This description referred only to what was merely the recognition of a *differentiation* in function, a differentiation made between the elders based on their gifting. That is, some elders devoted themselves *primarily* to preaching and teaching. Regrettably, this distinction led instead to the unbiblical creation of a third office, even "the first office of all," the "pastor."

Paul made this distinction in function clear: "The elders who *rule well* [lead, direct] are to be considered worthy of double honor, especially those who work hard at *preaching and teaching*" (1 Tim. 5:17; italics added). The apostle asserts that all elders *both* rule (lead[*]) and teach; this is also stated in the requirements for elders in Titus 1 and 1 Timothy 3. However, some elders are more gifted than others in leading or in teaching and, therefore, concentrate where God has gifted them. Because of this specialization, some of the early elders were primarily preachers-teachers. This confirms that there was a

---

[*] We will show later (p. 20) that "rule" is a misleading translation of *proïstēmi*.

division of labor among those who filled the office of elder, not different offices.

The English word "pastor" comes from the Latin word for "shepherd." The Greek word *poimēn,* translated either "pastor" or "shepherd," appears eighteen times in the New Testament. In nine instances, it refers to Jesus, where He is called a shepherd. In eight other cases, it refers to a literal shepherd. *Poimēn* is translated "shepherd" in all these places except Ephesians 4:11: "He gave some as apostles, and some as prophets, and some as evangelists, and some as *pastors* and teachers" (italics added). *This verse is the only mention of "pastor" in most English translations of the New Testament.* The word "pastor" does not show up in the other listings of roles and functions in the New Testament, and its use in translating Ephesians 4:11 has lamentably led to the invalid and unwarranted change from a functional description to an office.

In Ephesians 4:11, *poimēn* occurs with *didaskalos,* the term for "teacher"; unlike the proceeding gifts (that of apostle, prophet, and evangelist), in the Greek both words share a single article. Older commentators interpreted this as indicating that both words referred to the same person. This resulted in the "pastor-teacher" terminology. However, studies of all similar grammatical constructions in the New Testament and Greek literature show that reference to the same person can only be true if both nouns are singular and personal.

David B. Wallace, professor of New Testament Studies at Dallas Theological Seminary, wrote his Ph.D. dissertation at the same institution on this matter. Wallace states that the omission of the article in Ephesians 4:11 indicates that, rather than "pastor" and "teacher" being the same person, "one group overlaps with the other in some sense (either partial overlap for both, or one is a subset of the other). . . . The first group (pastors) belongs to the second group (teachers). That is, all who have the gift of pastor also would have the gift of teacher."[9] He points out that it is presumed that a man who has the gift of pastoring would also, but not necessarily, have the gift of teaching. But he says the reverse is not true: it is not true that all those gifted as teachers are gifted as pastors (shepherds).[10]

Even older commentators agree that Paul is referring to the gift (or gifts) rather than to a position or office. The verse asserts that the shepherding gift is to be expressed in part through teaching. Pastoring (Greek, *shepherding*) is required of all elders (1 Peter 5:1–2). All

---

* *KJV, RSV, NAS, NIV,* and *NASB,* among others.

15

elders must have the ability to teach. However, not all elders may be gifted as teachers. In a similar vein, all elders must shepherd even though only some are specifically gifted as shepherds.

The term "pastor" (shepherd) cannot be equated with, or be replaced with, the word "elder," since *poimēn* (like the English "shepherd") does not imply a "ruler" or "overseer"; it does not indicate status or a position. Therefore, Ephesians 4:11 cannot be used to state that *all* pastors (shepherds) are elders.

If Paul had intended that "pastor" be a distinct position in the church, it is inconceivable that he would *fail* to delineate the requirements for that position.

Paul spelled out explicit requirements for elders and deacons (1 Tim. 3:1–13; Titus 1:5–9). If he had intended that "pastor" be a distinct position in the church—which is for many now the most important position—it is inconceivable that Paul would *fail* to delineate the requirements for that position. Therefore, using the title "pastor" to distinguish that particular elder who is charged with the task of preaching-teaching from the other elders—especially those who are tent-making elders—conveys the wrong impression to the congregation and the watching world.

AN INVALID DISTINCTION

Probably the greatest threat to biblical elder leadership is the careless use of the term "pastor" to distinguish between those elders who preach and the other so-called "lay," tent-making elders.[*] Though designed to clarify roles, this separation—really an elevation of one type of elder and devaluation of another type of elder—actually results in confusion. Moreover, it creates two other serious difficulties: It sets up a division within the elder council, and it deprecates the efforts of the elders who have gifts other than preaching.

---

[*] Because the term "lay" implies two classes—"clergy" (elevated, having a special spiritual status), and "lay" or "laity" (second-class status), I do not use or endorse this terminology. However, some quotations cited herein contain this inappropriate terminology.

BIBLICAL ELDERSHIP

A professional seminary degree, or the practice called ordination, does not make a man who is called "pastor" *different* from others who are pastoring (that is, shepherding). The use of the title "Reverend" is an unbiblical attempt to elevate a professionally trained class to a priestly class.

**Probably the greatest threat to biblical elder leadership
is the careless use of the term "pastor."**

Both the Old Testament ("You shall be to Me a kingdom of priests and a holy nation," Ex. 19:6), and the New Testament ("But you are a chosen race, a royal priesthood, a holy nation, a people for God's own possession," 1 Peter 2:9), teach that all Christians are priests. Furthermore, Jesus *forbade* the use of elevating titles:

> "But do not be called Rabbi; for One is your Teacher, and you are all brothers. . . . Do not be called leaders [guides]; for One is your Leader, that is, Christ. But the greatest among you shall be your servant. Whoever exalts himself shall be humbled; and whoever humbles himself shall be exalted" (Matt. 23:8, 10–12).

Neither the custom of ordaining, meaning the conveying of or recognizing spiritual status or power, or the word "ordain" appear in the New Testament. Note that the words *poieō* (Mark 3:14), *kathistēmi* (Titus 1:5), *and cheirotoneō* (Acts 14:23) are translated in the King James version as "ordain", however most later versions translate them as "appoint," their true meaning.[*] Also, note that the New Testament practice of laying on of hands signified *only* the appointment to a specific assignment, as in the sending of Paul and Barnabas on the first missionary journey: "When they had fasted and prayed and laid their hands on them, they sent them away" (Acts 13:3). Retaining "pastor" as an honorific title to designate a man engaged in ministry full time is without biblical warrant and just perpetuates misconceptions.

When Paul went to the Jerusalem conference recorded in Acts 15 (also 16:4), the church leadership was listed as consisting of apostles and elders. In Acts 20, Paul called for the elders of the Ephesian church, and in Acts 21:18, he reported to the Apostle James and all

---

[*] *NAS, RSV, NIV, NASB, NKJV.*

the elders. In Philippians 1:1, Paul greeted "all the saints, . . . including the overseers and deacons." And in 1 Timothy, Paul instructed Timothy on the qualifications of elders and deacons. In any of these situations, where were the men we call "pastors" today? They were there: They were called elders! Obviously, this pastoring, that is, shepherding, and teaching of the local church, was provided by its elders, or overseers, not by a separate clergy.[*]

"Overseer" is not an additional office. Acts 20:17 and 28 make it clear that both the terms *episkopos,* "overseer" (sometimes translated *bishop*), and *presbyteros,* "elder," refer to the same position.[†] The term "overseer" refers to the function of the office, and the term "elder" emphasizes the spiritual maturity of the man (a seasoned shepherd) and the dignity of his office. (In the Old Testament, the word "elder" incorporated both connotations.) This conclusion is reinforced by Titus 1:7, where the term "overseer" is used in a passage that describes the qualifications of elders. In 1 Timothy 3:1–13, Paul lists the requirements to be fulfilled by men aspiring to be overseers; later in the letter (5:17), he refers to these same men as "elders." Finally, in 1 Peter 5:1–2, Peter charges the elders to *episkopeō,* "oversee," the church.

It is contrary to the teaching of Scripture to consider "pastor" and "elder" as separate offices.

While distinguishing between elders because of their areas of specialization is valid, it is contrary to the teaching of Scripture to consider "pastor" and "elder" as separate offices. Equally erroneous is the creation of the separate positions of "ruling elder" and "teaching elder," since all elders both lead and teach. The conclusion that "pastor" in Ephesians 4:11 refers to a function, rather than a position, is reinforced by Peter's direction that his fellow elders (all elders) be

---

[*] This does not imply that all "pastors," or those engaged in shepherding, are elders. Shepherding is a larger category. See pages 32–34, Who Governed the New Testament Churches?

[†] Note: 1 Timothy 4:14 refers to the elders collectively as *presbyterion.* The *KJV, NKJV, NASB,* and *NIV* translate *presbyterion* "presbytery," but this should not be confused with Presbyterians' usage of "presbytery" to refer to a hierarchical body over the local churches. This is not taught by, or implied by, 1 Timothy 4:14. Both Arndt and Gingrich, and Kittel and Friedrich give the meaning of *presbyterion* as a council of elders.[11]

involved in pastoring, that is, shepherding, the church (1 Peter 5:1–2). Paul issues the same instruction, "shepherd the church of God," to overseers (elders) in Acts 20:28.

In criticizing some uses of the title "pastor," I do not imply lack of honor for the high and valid calling and work to which many men have devoted their lives. And, to those faithful men who have long served under their calling as pastors, I again emphasize that I do not question their calling, only the terminology used to describe the calling. My argument is only with the use of a distinction that essentially devalues the high and valid calling and work of other elders.[*]

PLURALITY AND LEADERSHIP

As we have seen, Paul instructed Titus to "set in order what remains and appoint elders in every city as I directed you" (Titus 1:5). Notice that Paul and Peter did not intend the appointment of only one elder per church or city. As Acts 14:23 indicates, "They had appointed elders for them in every church"—in other words, *plural*, that is, *several* elders who were to shepherd and administer each early church. From this precedent the principle of a plurality of elders in each local church is established.

Some try to escape the implications of Acts 14:23 by saying that each house church had an elder, and that these elders functioned collectively at the city level. This sometimes may have been the case. A church in a small community may have operated only as a collection of house fellowships, and, therefore, that church had plural elders only in that sense. But the principle remains the same: Elders always acted collectively; their decisions were not made unilaterally, but were made *with* their brother elders. It simply cannot be argued that we may extrapolate from one elder presiding over a house church to a single elder (senior pastor) ruling a church of several hundred congregants today. The verse is explicit—"elders in every church." Therefore, whatever it is that constitutes a church, it is to be led by a plurality of elders.

---

[*] In describing the contemporary scene herein, at times the conventional practice of employing the word "pastor" to refer to the staff (salaried) preaching elder will be followed.

Paul is definite: Elders are not simply members of a board of directors, as they are in many churches today, but are men active in ministering among the people of the congregation. If Paul were to adjust to our contemporary church, he would have to advise: "Appreciate the Board that meets in secret and makes decisions for the congregation."

"They had appointed elders for them in every church"—in other words, *plural*, that is, *several* elders who were to shepherd and administer each early church.

What Paul did in fact ask for is: "But we request of you, brethren, that you appreciate those who diligently labor *among you*, and *have charge over you* in the Lord and *give you* instruction, and that you esteem them very highly in love because of their work" (1 Thess. 5:12–13, italics added). "Have charge over" is the translation of the same Greek word used in 1 Timothy 5:17, where Paul speaks of the elders who "rule" well. The Greek word *proïstēmi*, translated here as "rule," has the sense of leading by virtue of being out in front of or caring for others,[12] rather than leading by virtue of position, as does a king. Paul could have used the word *archō* (rule), but he did not. *Proïstēmi,* in contrast to *archō,* never implies a power relationship. Elders' authority is seen in their leading, teaching, and caring for God's household, not ever in domination, usurpation, or proud self-importance.

Hebrews 13:17 sets a standard for elder leadership that cannot be met by a board of directors that simply rubber stamps staff decisions: "Obey your leaders and submit to them, for they keep watch over your souls as those who will give account." This picture of intimate, vital care, "watch over your souls," is reinforced by the choice of the Greek word *peithō*, which is translated here "obey." It means, "Let yourselves be convinced or persuaded by."[13] Thus we have the picture of elders lovingly persuading the flock through teaching, not by handing down decisions.

Jesus Christ is the Head of the church. In order to honor His preeminence in the way we operate and also be obedient to the Apostle Paul's specific directions, we need to put in place the correct biblical structure to govern our local church. Most churches say they acknowledge the headship of Christ. In actual governance, however, not many adhere to the principle that each elder is *directly responsible to Christ*, and never to a chairman, or moderator, or to a senior pastor. Paul's behavior is consistent with his assertion that the Head of the church is Christ. He never, by precept or example, singles out one elder as having authority over other elders. Therefore, to be true to the teaching of the New Testament, the local church and its elder council must function in such a manner that these two truths—*the supreme headship of Christ and the equality of all elders*—are honored and demonstrated in practice, not just in principle.

This brief study substantiates the claim that the three fundamental and nonnegotiable aspects of truly biblical church governance are:

- The plurality of the elders

- The equality of those elders who are responsible for preaching with their fellow elders, in both *principle* and practice

- The essential, integral involvement of the elders in the leadership of all of the church's ministries

These three elements are permanent features of the biblical church. The elimination of any one component causes basic deviation from the apostles' intent for the church. Of course, the three indispensable fundamentals may differ in appearance as each church works out its response to its local culture, but they must be present in essence. As we examine how our churches can be governed biblically, we will see clearly that obedience to the New Testament directives unlocks great reservoirs of talent and initiative within our congregations. In fact, it already has.

He is . . . the head of the body, the church.
Colossians 1:18

Chapter 2

Biblical Governance

AT THIS POINT, it will be profitable to state my major premises. These are the premises which will regulate this discussion of the practical aspects of achieving biblical governance and leadership of the church. First, because we are committed to the authority of the Word, we must begin by determining exactly what were the instructions and practice of the New Testament period. After that, we can judge which current practices are the valid adaptations to our present culture. They will be those that preserve the apostles' intent. Some issues will be settled by the unambiguous and indisputable teaching of the Word. Other conclusions will be derived by logical implication from those clear teachings. However, not all details of church governance are plainly taught or implied by Scripture. For guidance in these instances, the leadership of each church must use its best judgment, informed by the general teaching of the Word, while being careful to preserve the functions and essential character of the New Testament church.* Consequently, I have avoided any assertions, except those explicitly mandated by Scripture, that would be considered denominational distinctives.

---

* J. P. Moreland, professor of philosophy at Talbot School of Theology, who agrees that plurality of elders is an absolute mandate for the church, also stresses the need to distinguish between forms and functions: "We need to make a careful distinction between forms and functions in the church. A New Testament function is an absolute mandate that every church must do. . . . By contrast, a form is a culturally relative means of fulfilling biblical functions. Forms are valuable as a means to accomplish those functions and should be constantly evaluated, kept, or replaced in light of their effectiveness. Examples of forms are the existence of youth directors, Sunday school classes, [and the like]."[14]

22

BIBLICAL GOVERNANCE

Second, I categorically ascribe to a thoroughly biblical form of church governance. This being the case, uncritical assimilation of secular management principles is rejected. However, there is much that can be learned from studies of management methods. It is unwise to ignore the empirical research on the effect of individual and group behavior on their served constituencies. Many of the advances that have occurred in the development of church organizations have been proper and beneficial.

The church as a whole is plagued by the fact that each of us is guilty to varying degrees of sinful behavior. Students of organizational theory are well aware of the destructive repercussions of untrammeled self-interest, although they would never define such conduct in biblical terminology. Many studies have assessed the effectiveness of various organizational structures and practices in restricting the self-interested conduct of individuals and groups in order to benefit those they serve. On the other hand, it is necessary to examine the negative consequences for the church of some business and government methods we have appropriated for church management—methods that are inimical to the welfare of the church because they work at cross-purposes to its true nature. Above all, we must be careful to understand and preserve the apostles' intentions. Traditions embedded in our churches, our culture, and modern business practices must not obscure the vision for the church set forth in Scripture.

Traditions embedded in our churches, our culture, and modern business practices must not obscure the vision for the church set forth in Scripture.

The third premise is that a church's true nature is accurately expressed in the working relationships practiced among its leadership. We will look at the connections between elders—that is, the elders as a governing group, the church's staff, and, especially, those responsible for filling the pulpit, the preachers. How each person or group views himself (or themselves) and works with the others (or works unilaterally) controls the health of the church. How the preacher regards himself (or the preachers think of themselves) in relationship to the church's elders will be conducive either to godly, biblical church government, or to ineffective or destructive governance. Therefore, all aspects of these associations must be addressed.

The Challenge

Opposition to biblical governance, overt or covert, comes from many quarters. Despite our sincere efforts to be faithful to the biblical directives on church governance, we are all confronted with trends in the present culture. Today, many evangelical congregations are immersed in an environment and setting radically different from that encountered by the early church. We must embrace some changes wrought by time as beneficial, and declare others to be in opposition to God's revealed will for us. As always, discernment is necessary in forming biblical views on marriage, divorce, parenting, the roles of men and women, and the like, that speak to our contemporaries. Equally important is the task of separating wheat from chaff as we evaluate both the incursions into the governance of the church of societal and institutional values, and any necessary and valid accommodations of New Testament practices to our culture.

Just as Christian marriage and family have somewhat different expressions today, compared to their presentation in Paul's time, the governing of today's churches will appear to be different. However, as in our marriages and families, where their essential characteristics are concerned, our churches must remain faithful to the biblical teachings, and must be structured and led to reflect those characteristics.

An additional issue compels us to look carefully at the leadership of the church. It is generally expected that when a church is in a community that has only a small percentage of evangelicals—as is true of most churches—that body should be experiencing significant growth. However, many churches with leaders who strive to remain uncompromising in their obedience to the Word—including governance by a plurality of elders—fail to see growth. Why is this the case? I believe that the answer lies in two things: the inadequate concept of the role of the elders; and the failure to establish an elder-leadership culture that is consistent with the New Testament directives, instead of one shaped by historical precedent or cultural expectations.

The church growth movement is replete with advice on how to grow a church into a "megachurch." These writings and conference presentations are primarily based on individual success stories. Nevertheless, the advice proffered rarely refers to either Jesus' or the apostles' explicit directions for the church, and, in fact, often postulates practices contrary to the biblical model.

From those churches that have experienced significant growth one hears a different—still sad—but consistent story. Leaders corroborate (and I have witnessed) the same scenario: the distressing loss of a church plant's or a small church's essential biblical character, once prized at the beginning, as it matures into a "successful" church. Does this have to be? Is it not possible for a church to flourish, meeting the needs of its congregation and the surrounding population, and still maintain its biblical distinctives and leadership? Surely we are able to emulate the precedents set forth in Scripture, and resist the pressure to replace biblical leadership with borrowings from the secular or corporate world.

NEW TESTAMENT PERSPECTIVE ON LEADERSHIP

Let us begin with an examination of the biblical teaching on leadership. Scripture does not give us detailed specifications—say, a convenient, succinct set of directives from Paul—to be reproduced in each church's bylaws. However, the New Testament unquestionably provides our Lord's own example, His directions to the disciples, the apostles' personal examples and instructions, the workings of the early elder governing bodies or councils, and the involvement of their congregations in decision-making. Examination of these passages, with careful attention to the context, will yield derived biblical principles for implementing elder leadership overall, and for conducting the work of the elder council in particular.

As we would expect, Jesus—the Sovereign God incarnate—was plainly in charge in the discharge of His earthly ministry and in His training of the twelve disciples. He did not request the disciples' advice before making decisions, and even chastised them for offering unsolicited, often worldly, opinions (Matt. 16:23; John 13:8). As the Head of the Church, Jesus rightfully commands His Church. His decision-making did not involve consulting His disciples. Therefore, we must be careful in applying this aspect of His example to the leadership of our churches. He is the Sovereign God, the "Head of the body, the church" (Col. 1:18). No man is. No men are.

However, Christ never acted alone. In keeping with the triune nature of the Godhead, He proclaimed that all His decisions were made in concert with God the Father: "I can do nothing on My own initiative. . . . because I do not seek My own will, but the will of Him who sent Me" (John 5:30; cf. 14:10, 24; 5:19; 17:8). He undertook nothing on His own authority and was diligent in stating this precedent to his disciples.

25

JESUS' TEACHING ON LEADERSHIP

The disciples' training and development by the Lord is part of Christ's example that we are to emulate. While He was with them, He led them to work together as a group. Even when he sent them out to preach, He sent them by two's (Mark 6:7–13). Nor did Jesus single out one disciple for special preparation for assuming His place after His departure, but chose to continue His ministry through the disciples. After His resurrection, Jesus instructed the men to remain together until Pentecost. In fact, most of the disciples stayed together in Jerusalem until the church there was well established through their collective efforts. Jesus had taught them to function *collectively*, not as individuals.

**The Lord commanded the twelve to function
as *equals*, and to serve one another.**

In addition, the Lord commanded the twelve to function as *equals*, and to serve one another. He carried out a dramatic demonstration of this principle by washing their feet (John 13:1–15). That act is intentionally preserved in the Word for our instruction. The Lord further emphasized the disciples' equality and lack of rank by condemning any attempt on their part to exert privilege or authority over each other. James and John were sharply rebuked for wanting places of honor in the kingdom (Mark 10:35–45), and the disciples were warned that they must not emulate Gentile rulers in their exercise of authority:

> Calling them to Himself, Jesus said to them, . . . "But it is not this way among you, but whoever wishes to become great among you shall be your servant; and whoever wishes to be first among you shall be slave of all. For even the Son of Man did not come to be served, but to serve, and to give His life a ransom for many" (Mark 10:42–45).

Jesus also contrasted the conduct He required of His disciples with the behavior of the Pharisees:

> Then Jesus spoke to the crowds and to His disciples, saying: "The scribes and the Pharisees . . . . love the place of honor at banquets and the chief seats in the synagogues, and respectful greetings in the market places, and being called

Rabbi by men. But do not be called Rabbi; for One is your Teacher, and you are all brothers. Do not call anyone on earth your father; for One is your Father, He who is in heaven. Do not be called leaders; for One is your Leader,* that is, Christ. But the greatest among you shall be your servant. Whoever exalts himself shall be humbled; and whoever humbles himself shall be exalted" (Matt. 23:1–2, 6–12).

In this passage, Jesus specifically forbids the disciples—and all those who will follow in their shepherding-teaching ministry in the church—to take on positions or titles of *individual power* or *authority*. This does not mean that men are not permitted to lead. We see Peter, Paul, James, and many others, all leading at various times. However, they did not direct the disciples by demanding their respect due to some hierarchical positions they supposedly held. These teachers, preachers, church planters, and shepherd-elders guided others and took responsibility by virtue of their gifting, with respect to the issue at hand and God's calling.

Peter was no exception to this rule. Note that Jesus' statement to Peter about binding and loosing (Matt. 16:19) was delivered in response to Peter's confession of Jesus' messianic identity. Plainly, He did not set Peter apart (to exercise this authority), as if Peter were an exception to the equality of the other leaders, because Matthew records that this exact prerogative was granted to the *whole* church (18:18). In this case, Jesus is giving instructions about how discipline should take place in the church.

When individual intervention and confrontation by two or more witnesses fail, the matter is to be brought before the congregation; if the offending person refuses to listen to the church, he is to be disfellowshipped and treated as a non-Christian. This is the context in which Jesus repeats the same words He had spoken previously to Peter: "Truly I say to you, whatever you bind on earth shall have been bound in heaven; and whatever you loose on earth shall have been loosed in heaven" (Matt. 18:18). Without doubt, Peter's faith relationship to Christ empowered him, not some so-called position.

---

* The issue here is not the use of the word "leader" as a function, but as a title. The point is, if Christ is our Leader, no *man* can occupy His position.

BIBLICAL GOVERNANCE

THE APOSTLES' TEACHING ON LEADERSHIP

The apostle Paul speaks of the church as "having been built on the foundation of the apostles and prophets, Christ Jesus Himself being the cornerstone" (Eph. 2:20). He teaches that the church has a singular Head, Christ, but that it was established and built on the foundation set in place by the Old Testament prophets[*] and the New Testament apostles. The apostles were ever mindful of their collective experience with Jesus during His three years of ministry on earth. Moreover, they came from a people whose heritage included being led by a plurality of elders who were directly responsible to God.

Collective Responsibility

Israel, under God's direction, had transitioned from unitary rule under Moses (who, in his role, foreshadowed Christ), to collective leadership by elders and judges who were directly responsible to God. Later, when Israel rebelled against being a nation led by God and asked for a king, the prophet Samuel declared that, in so doing, Israel had rejected God. The people had said: "'Now appoint a king for us to judge us like all the nations.'. . . [and] The Lord said to Samuel, 'Listen to the voice of the people in regard to all that they say to you, for they have not rejected you, but they have rejected Me from being king over them'" (1 Sam. 8:5, 7). Sadly, the period of the kings was not the last time in the history of God's dealings with His people that the grievous error was made of interposing an authority between God and the elders who were charged with ruling.

The apostles taught the principle of elder leadership of the church by precept and by example. A review of how the apostles conducted church affairs illustrates this. Though each apostle possessed full apostolic authority, Scripture records that their use of this authority was sparing. A few examples of the apostles making independent decisions—independent of their peers, not of the Lord—are:

- Peter's dealing with Ananias and Sapphira (Acts 5:1–11)

---

[*] Some argue that, in this verse, the word "prophets" refers to New Testament prophets because of the word order. However, in either case, establishment of the church was a collective effort.

- Peter's decision to stay at Cornelius's house (Acts 10:1–48)

- Paul's decision to travel separately from Barnabas, over the issue of John Mark (Acts 15:36–41)

- Paul's decision to circumcise Timothy (Acts 16:1–3)

- Paul's decision that the church should excommunicate an immoral "so-called brother" (1 Cor. 5:1–13)

While the apostles had the authority to administer matters in this fashion, that is, as authorities over *all* the churches, this was not their usual mode of operation. Their usual mode is demonstrated in 1 Thessalonians 2:4–7, where Paul says that he exhorts the believers in a gentle manner, "even though as apostles of Christ we might have asserted our authority" (v. 6). In fact, the apostles never acted unilaterally as the heads of individual churches. They preferred to support the elders and the churches in making decisions. For example, in defending his decision concerning the Gentile believer Cornelius before the other apostles and brethren in Jerusalem, Peter did not claim apostolic privilege. He presented the facts and his reasoning so the brothers would be able to concur with his conclusion (Acts 11:1–18).

Likewise, Paul apparently took the step of explaining to the church at Antioch his decision to travel without Barnabas and John Mark, and received their blessing on his trip (Acts 15:40). Also, when criticized for not requiring Gentiles to be circumcised, Paul put the matter before the apostles and elders in Jerusalem. In this instance, Paul did not assert apostolic prerogative; he stated his case and then stepped back to allow the church to decide the issue (Acts 15:1–35).[*] In fact, the Jerusalem Council will be scrutinized in greater detail later, because the description of its functioning offers us a model structure and procedure for deciding church issues.

---

[*] Paul did not assert his apostolic prerogatives in a private meeting prior to the public meeting. The overwhelming evidence is with the position explained by F. F. Bruce, who ascribes the description, in Galatians 2:1–10, to a *private* meeting between Paul, James, Peter, and John in Jerusalem which occurred on an earlier visit (detailed in Acts 11:27–30), rather than to one preceding the *public* meeting of Acts 15:1–35.[15]

BIBLICAL GOVERNANCE

The apostles handled most situations by encouraging the elders and the congregation to come to decisions through consensus-producing effort, "after . . . much debate" (Acts 15:7), and "with the whole church" (Acts 15:22). Examples of such collective decisions and actions supported by the apostles were:

- Appointing Judas's replacement (Acts 1:15–26)

- Choosing of the seven to care for widows (Acts 6:1–6)

- Distributing the relief offering sent to the church in Judea by its elders (not by the apostles; Acts 11:27–30)

- Commissioning of Barnabas and Saul (Acts 13:1–3)

- Laying hands on Timothy (1 Tim. 4:14)

- Anointing the sick (James 5:14–15)

Paul rightly understood that following a single leader constituted an attack on, actually a denial of, the headship of Christ and the unity of the church, and met the issue head on: "Each of you is saying, 'I am of Paul,' and 'I of Apollos,' and 'I of Cephas,' and 'I of Christ.' Has Christ been divided?" (1 Cor. 1:12–13). Here the apostle dealt directly with all attempts by the people to interpose any leader between themselves and Christ and thereby fragment the local church. The most egregious error committed here is by those who said "I [am] of Christ." These people wanted no accountability. They were making themselves the sole judges of Christ's will for the church.

Paul warns the man tempted to be a sole leader "not to think more highly of himself than he ought to think; . . . We have many members in one body and all the members do not have the same function" (Rom. 12:3–5). Paul goes on here (vv. 6–7), and in three other passages, to stress that multiple gifts were bestowed on the church, and that the church is made complete through the combined efforts of believers exercising these gifts, not through one person exercising all of them (1 Cor. 12:8–11, 28–31; Eph. 4:11–13).

BIBLICAL GOVERNANCE

Unity Urged, but not Always Possible

The apostles urged unity, just as had Christ. They taught that shepherd-elders were to serve with a common purpose, and were to be of one accord. Paul's instruction echoed the words of David in the Psalms, "Behold, how good and how pleasant it is for brothers to dwell together in unity!" (Ps.133:1), and Christ's prayer, "that they may all be one" (John 17:21).

Consider Paul's counsel to the church—and, by implication, for its leadership—on unity: "Now I exhort you, brethren, by the name of our Lord Jesus Christ, that you all agree and that there be no divisions among you, but that you be made complete in the same mind and in the same judgment" (1 Cor. 1:10). Paul condemned jealousy and strife as "fleshly," the behavior of "mere men" (1 Cor. 3:3), and he entreated the church: "Make my joy complete by being of the same mind, maintaining the same love, united in spirit, intent on one purpose" (Phil. 2:2). Having previously taught his protégé Timothy that all elders must be temperate, and not pugnacious (1 Tim. 3:2–3), Paul also instructed the young elder and apostolic legate: "The Lord's bond-servant must not be quarrelsome, but be kind to all, . . . patient when wronged, with gentleness correcting those who are in opposition" (2 Tim. 2:24–25). The apostle John expressed the same desire that "fellow workers" be servant leaders, not like Diotrephes; John criticized this man, "who loves to be first among them [the leaders, and] does not accept what we say" (3 John 8–9). And last, but not least, is Peter, who demonstrated how well he had adopted the role of servant leadership as he was exhorting the churches' elders. He spoke of himself as "your fellow elder," rather than reminding them that he held the position of apostle (1 Peter 5:1).

However, while the apostles urged unity and accord, they recognized this would not always be the case in the church. In Acts 20:28–31, we are forewarned to expect that unity in governing bodies will be challenged and thwarted. Paul strictly admonished the Ephesian elders—and us—that rogue elders will rise up from within elder councils and attempt to split them and their churches. Even the original twelve disciples had a Judas. Moreover, between the two extremes of harmony and rebellion there lies a continuum of minor-to-severe forms of disunity. As a consequence, while always seeking agreement, elders must be prepared to take positions and make decisions (which some will label as divisive), in order to protect the church.

BIBLICAL GOVERNANCE

Does Collective Responsibility Abrogate Leadership?

How does Paul's conduct square with our present-day, research-based understanding of effective leadership? Stephen P. Robbins, author of the most widely used textbook on organizational behavior, defines leadership as, "The ability to influence a group toward the achievement of goals."[16] He cites Warren Bennis's study of ninety of the most effective and successful leaders in the United States. Bennis found that they had four common competencies:

- The leaders "had a compelling vision or sense of purpose."

- The leaders "could communicate that vision in clear terms that their followers could readily identify with."

- The leaders "demonstrated consistency and focus in the pursuit of their vision."

- The leaders "knew their own strengths and capitalized on them."[17]

Clearly, the apostle Paul was this kind of leader. Collective responsibility through plurality of elders does not in any way take away from the vital need and ample opportunity for elders to provide effective biblical leadership. How this ought to look in the church today will be discussed later.

WHO GOVERNED THE NEW TESTAMENT CHURCHES?

At this point, we have established: First, that *the elders* were not only preachers in the New Testament churches, but also providers of sustained shepherding for each congregation (Titus 1:5); and second, that the apostle Paul mandated that every local church be governed by *a plurality of these elders* (a group of several, Acts 14:23). Therefore, understanding that a plurality of elders exercised authority in the New Testament churches, we must next determine who composed that governing plurality.

Paul's exhortation on double honor—"The elders who rule [lead, direct] well are to be considered worthy of double honor, especially those who work hard at preaching and teaching" (1 Tim. 5:17)—sets the precedent. He explicitly urges that some elders, especially those who were gifted in teaching and preaching and had dedicated themselves to these tasks, were to be supported financially by the church. Paul's clear teaching is that the double honor consists of honor and respect, *and* wages: such a "laborer is worthy of his wages" (v. 18). This financial support freed these elders to devote greater time and energy to their responsibilities. Other New Testament elders—bivocational elders who supported themselves—were also to be honored and respected, and should continue to be so today. Ever since, these men have been referred to as *tentmakers*, after Paul's own method of self-support, the craft of tentmaking. Both types of elders governed side-by-side and constituted the elderships of the early churches. The epistles teach that these elders had multiple functions: They were all *shepherds* of the congregation (1 Peter 5:1–2); they all *taught* (all lists of elder qualifications include the ability to teach, and Paul adds exhorting and refuting, Titus 1:9), and they all shared in the governance *of the churches* ("have charge over you in the Lord," 1 Thess. 5:12–13).

**All elders shared in the governance
of the New Testament churches.**

The fact that some New Testament elders performed the function of the modern-day "pastor" does not mean that all present-day "pastors" are elders. The term "pastor" is not precise, and "shepherd" is a broad term. A twenty-five-year old seminary graduate who has never previously served in a church is called a "pastor" in some churches. Youth and children's directors, neither of whom have oversight responsibility for the whole church, are often called "pastors." This ambiguous use of the term results from forcing it to designate both a function and an office. Churches have taken the *description* of shepherding, that is pastoring, and made it into a title or an "office" in the church. (Shepherding is a broad category. It can be undertaken by anyone, regardless of age, gender, or fixed qualifications.) Therefore, when it is asserted that all elders are shepherds, it is not the same as saying that all those engaged in shepherding are elders.

The New Testament also mentions other gifted men who served multiple churches as representatives of the apostles, as evangelists, and as church planters, but these men were not responsible for the long-term governance of the individual churches. The elders—"Those who diligently labor among you, and have charge over you in the Lord and give you instruction" (1 Thess. 5:12)—governed the churches.

33

Paul's insistence that all elders be able to teach and to confront error, as unique requirements of their office, is consistent with his own use of *teaching* as the primary means of exercising authority, that is, governing the church.[*] The elder must "be able both to exhort in sound doctrine and to refute those who contradict. For there are many rebellious men, empty talkers and deceivers . . . who must be silenced" (Titus 1:9–11). To be honest, at times each of us has been tempted to wish he could dispatch a problem in the church with the speed with which Peter dealt with Ananias and Sapphira (Acts 5:1–11). However, the authority of elders is exercised primarily through the teaching of biblical truth, and rarely through exerting power. When Hebrews 13:17 speaks of the congregation's obedience to the church's leadership, the word *peithō* is used for obey. This choice of *peithō* focuses on the primacy of teaching: it means to obey in the sense of letting oneself be convinced or persuaded.

THE ESTABLISHMENT OF COLLEGIATE GOVERNANCE

Why did the apostles establish the standard of governance of the church by a plurality of elders, with the resulting, vital necessity for collegiate—that is, collectively considered—decisions? Three reasons are unmistakable. First, the apostles followed much of Jewish tradition, including leadership by a plurality of elders serving under God. Second, the apostles foresaw a grave danger ahead for the growing church. Paul explicitly forewarned the elders that the church would be infected by sin and composed of fallible men, and that false elders, teachers, and prophets would infiltrate the elders themselves: "Savage wolves will come in among you, not sparing the flock; and from among your own selves men will arise speaking perverse things, to draw away the disciples [members of the congregation] after them" (Acts 20:29–30).

It stands to reason that the church will be most secure if it is entrusted to the care of *multiple* elders—elders who are holding each other accountable in centering on God's will. It will be much safer

---

[*] Teaching (in the context of the early church, house churches then being prevalent) cannot necessarily be equated with the gifting required to fill the pulpit of a large church; and, therefore, the ability to teach from the pulpit cannot be a required qualification for one's being an elder.

than if left in the hands of one man or a few men who are not held accountable, and who may be inclined to arbitrary or dictatorial leadership. Learning of, and focusing on, the Chief Shepherd's will for the church is made more certain if the leadership is committed to the principle of collegiate leadership, because *God uses the interaction of the plurality to surface and clarify His will.* In fact, the Holy Spirit's work is demonstrated through the consensus He draws supernaturally from leaders of diverse backgrounds and gifts.

It stands to reason that the church will be most secure if it is entrusted to the care of *multiple* elders—elders who are holding each other accountable.

The third reason for the establishment of collegiate governance was Paul's belief that God had blessed the church with—and the church required—leaders possessing a variety of gifts. It appears he understood the fact, now being widely recognized, that one man, in and of himself, cannot possess all the competencies (gifts) required to lead a church. J. P. Moreland asserts:

> The local church should be led and taught by a plurality of voices called elders, and these voices should be equal. . . . No one person has enough gifts, perspective, and maturity to be given the opportunity disproportionately to shape the personality and texture of a local church.[18]

Warren Bennis finds this to be true even in the secular world. He comments on collaboration in the world of business and social institutions in his book *Organizing Genius*:

> In our constantly changing, global, highly technological society, collaboration is a necessity. The Lone Ranger, the incarnation of the individual problem solver, is dead. In his place, we have a new model for creative achievement: The Great Group.[19]

In *The Power of Team Leadership: Finding Strength in Shared Responsibility*, George Barna, founder of Barna Research Group, an opinion polling firm that serves the Christian community,[*] lists the four essential leadership approaches that are critical to a church's leadership:[20] the directing leader, the strategic leader, the team-builder leader, and the operational leader. Barna expands:

> Because each of these approaches to leadership requires a different way of viewing reality, a different type of relationship with people, and a distinct set of skills within the leadership domain, it is not possible for any one individual to be the "complete" leader. In fact, if you possessed all four of these aptitudes, the best description of you might be "clinically schizophrenic." You would always be at war with yourself as you strive to see the world from disparate points of view.[21]
>
> We found that even the greatest leaders usually possess just one of the four aptitudes. That does not mean that they are incompetent or incomplete leaders; it is simply a recognition that leadership is so demanding and complex that no one individual can do all aspects of leadership to perfection.[22]

BIBLICAL PRINCIPLES

The New Testament directives allow great latitude in the expression of elder leadership—in elders fulfilling their responsibilities to shepherd and maintain order in the church. However, from the perspective of the New Testament passages pertaining to leadership that we have just examined, general principles emerge. We must adhere to these if we are to represent ourselves as biblical, and if we expect God to help us do our job well, that is, in a godly and

---

[*] The opinions of the Barna Research Group are important because they are informed by significant polling data. Barna's books, *Habits of Highly Effective Churches* (Ventura, Calif.: Issachar Resources, 1998), and *The Power of Team Leadership* (Colorado Springs, Co.: WaterBrook Press, 2001), both address the shortcomings of clergy-led, hierarchical churches, and, as such, are valuable and recommended. Regrettably, when he suggests remediation for lack of success, Barna's approaches compensates for the weaknesses of these organizations, rather than suggesting the adoption of a thoroughly biblical standard. His uncritical acceptance of aspects of the modern milieu—the clergy-laity division, a preeminent senior pastor role, and gender-neutral roles—limits the applicability of his otherwise valid insights.

productive manner. How presumptuous of us to expect the prospering of our efforts if we are unwilling to shed our ecclesiastical cultures and to adopt biblically derived standards.

Prior to looking into how the plurality of elders, in the form of an elder council, might best govern, let me explain that, for clarity on the vocabulary used herein, I will follow Alexander Strauch's usage in *Biblical Eldership*:

> By definition, the elder structure of [church] government is a collective form of leadership in which each elder shares equally the position, authority, and responsibility. There are different names for this type of leadership structure. More formally, it is called collective, corporate, or collegiate leadership. In contemporary terms, it is referred to as multiple church leadership, plurality, shared leadership, or team leadership.[23]

Moreover, many who are committed to biblical eldership also prefer the term, *elder council*, rather than "elder board," for referring to the governing body of the church: *council* is a New Testament term, (used twenty-three times to refer to the Jewish elders), and *board* has the secular connotations of a corporate board of directors, with all its attendant power relationships. In summary, as we have seen from our study thus far, these biblical principles for the conduct of elder governance have been established:

- Christ is head of the church, and, therefore, head of the elder council: "He is . . . the head of the body, the church" (Col. 1:18).

- No one, including a pastor or pastors, may be placed in a position of power or authority over individual elders, or the council, thereby usurping the position of Christ. This follows from the first principle. Also, it is invalid to use the authority structure of *God - Moses - the elders - the people* as precedence for the authority structure of *God - pastor - the elders - the congregation*, since Moses prefigured Christ, not the pastors.

- Elders are individually answerable to Christ and to the collective body of elders (the council). This follows from the first principle, since no one, including a pastor, may rule over the elders. The pastor or moderator may only serve as one of them: "Be on guard for *yourselves*" (Acts 20:28, italics added).

- Decisions are to be made collegially. This is established by the precedent of Acts 15. Since all are answerable to Christ, and not to any other substitute leader, the collective seeking of Christ's will for the church is required.

- Unity is always desired but not always achieved. For example, Paul and Barnabas disagreed on taking John Mark along on their trip to revisit and strengthen the churches (Acts 15:39).

- The task of the moderator of the council is to encourage accord, never to rule the council or make unilateral decisions (the extension of the second principle).

- Leadership is task-specific, temporary, and based on gifting and God's calling. It is always the result of the other elders' recognition of God's gifting of the designated man, not the result of a hierarchical order or status in a power structure.

- The elder council exercises its biblical authority over the church primarily through teaching: Elders must "be able both to exhort in sound doctrine and to refute those who contradict" (Titus 1:9); "Appreciate those [elders] who diligently labor among you, and have charge over [lead] you in the Lord and give you instruction" (1 Thess. 5:12).

DISTORTIONS OF THE BIBLICAL MODEL

Before delving into how a biblical council of elders should function, I am constrained to point out that this form of leadership is not the norm these days. Sadly, the biblical model was perverted early in church history, as church bodies and systems moved to accommodate to secular cultures, and the governing structures of many of our modern-day churches perpetuate these man-centered distortions. The following classification of organizational types will help us understand the degree of deformation.

Those who study organizations categorize them as either hierarchical or horizontal. In a hierarchical organization, the authority and responsibility for decision-making is held by one person or an oligarchy of strong individuals. In contrast, according to Michael Doyle and David Straus, authors of *How to Make Meetings Work:*

The New Interaction Method, "in horizontal groups and organizations, the authority and responsibility for decisions rest with a specific group of people; final decisions can only be made by the vote (or the consensus) of a quorum."[24] The tenets of the New Testament clearly place the church's governance in the horizontal organization category. There were no senior pastors or chief elders in the New Testament church. Christ is still the Chief Shepherd (1 Peter 2:25; 5:4) of the church, and, as elders or pastors, we must not infringe on that position. The question is, in our present context, how may we confirm that our particular church is modeling the New Testament precedent?

LEADERSHIP BY ONE OR AN OLIGARCHY

At the outset, if a church has a lead or senior pastor, assessment of his role is crucial in determining the degree to which that body follows the New Testament model for church governance. Yes, we do find those biblically governed churches which function well, each with a single preacher, but these are men who have no hierarchical ambitions. Whether they are the founding or sole pastors or not is overridden by their unqualified belief in the equality of all elders.

On the other hand, often a senior (lead) pastor (he may be the founding pastor) simply directs the church with the passive acquiescence of a supportive board and congregation. Other churches are ruled by senior pastors, aided by small groups of powerful men who are not necessarily *true elders.* True elders are those men actually involved in ministry, actively engaged in shepherding the church.

DEMOCRACY

At the opposite extreme from churches experiencing one-man rule, or government by a compliant oligarchy, are those bodies which, through congregational rule, espouse the democratic principle by which each member supposedly has an equal vote in the governance of the church. However, besides being unsupported by Scripture, pure democracy seldom functions in practice. Churches with a congregational form of government do not meet every time a management decision is required. Instead, the congregation delegates most matters of leadership to a lead pastor, a few individuals, or a board.

ELDER-LED IN NAME ONLY

Further, often where it exists in name, elder governance may not appear as intended in the New Testament. In the history of the church and in current church practice, the proper functioning of the elders has been largely abandoned. Shortly after the apostolic period, the governance of the church was corrupted by the borrowing of secular constructs from pagan governments, the military, and, much later, from the modern-day corporate world. Today, an elder board is likely to operate in a fashion analogous to that of a corporate board of directors. The members of the board have been put there because of their *external* reputation or expertise, not because of their *internal* involvement in ministering in and shepherding the church. The board exists to be a check and balance to the staff, or simply as the senior pastor's rubber stamp. Either form is a substantial departure, having no resemblance to the apostles' dictums.

The organizational charts of many churches reveal that, despite a supposed commitment to elder leadership, they, in fact, have boards of directors. The elders are shown at the top of the organization, with everyone else reporting to the elders. So far so good. However, a staff layer is inserted between the elders and the ministries. In almost every case, the staff layer is under the direction of a senior or executive pastor and the ministries are led by paid employees, thereby downgrading the elders' status to that held by a mere passive board of directors.

**Biblical eldership cannot in fact exist
successfully in a church that does not have
a biblical leadership culture.**

This situation is not surprising because biblical eldership cannot in fact exist successfully in a church that does not have a biblical leadership culture. In genuine elder governance, council members do not simply watch ("support") a paid staff from a distance.

True elders are actively engaged in ministry. They are men "who diligently labor among you, and have charge over you" (1 Thess. 5:12). Barna comments on the fallacy in this situation, calling it "congregational dependence on staff":

> In tens of thousands of multi-staff churches, the staff members are viewed as the ministers: When ministry must be done, it is assigned to staff, who must then cajole congregants to get involved, as necessary. In fact, our

research indicates that most Protestant pastors see growth in the number of paid staff as an indicator of church health and good leadership.[25]

PSEUDO-TEAM APPROACHES

Another deviation from true biblical leadership shows up in those administrations that actually claim to exhibit a team approach. Frequently, a little inside investigation reveals several internal procedures that belie the assertion. First, and tragically, because of the highly visible position of elders responsible for preaching (usually paid staff), the attitudes and vocabulary they employ when referring to the other elders will either endorse and support the principle of biblical leadership, or prevent or destroy it. If preachers think that they are a continuation of the Old Testament priesthood (in violation of the priesthood of all believers) by asking that they be referred to as pastors—in contrast to the other elders—biblical eldership and leadership cannot be said to exist. However, again we must remember that the question should not be of title, but rather of relationship to other elders.

Second, staff may have carved out personal fiefdoms in which their initiatives are only subject to their own or staff approval. This same staff may claim that they have behaved in this manner because the other elders are "not engaged," and that is probably accurate. The truth is that the elders' reaction is attributable to the *atmosphere* that has been created. Seeing the lay of the land, elders who are busy men with careers and families are not going to make the sacrifice of time and effort to rubber-stamp initiatives after decisions have already been made by paid staff.

In fact, by their actions, such staff are either preventing the team from succeeding or destroying an existing team. Their behavior demotivates the excluded team members, and demonstrates that staff are not really committed to the equality of elders. We cannot accept their claim to be team players, because they actually eschew true teamwork in which the participants desire, and insist on, bringing all members of the team on board during the formulation of an initiative.

Even when elder governance is the supposed management standard, failure not only to define the biblical roles of those responsible for preaching—but also those of the elders and the congregation—leads to de facto aberrations. Some structures we have put in place are a far cry from the governance established in the New Testament. All of us should honestly and carefully examine how we are governing our churches. Have we participated in this slide away from the biblical model?

CAN THE NEW TESTAMENT MODEL WORK TODAY?

Many agree in principle with what is set forth here about the New Testament church, but they complain that such a form of government—leadership by the council of elders, a team of equals—is impractical in this day and age, and cannot possibly work. In fact, they are right about one thing: biblical eldership cannot coexist with a distorted, unbiblical understanding of the roles of the elders and those called pastors.

DESIRE FOR A KING

Initially, skeptics argue that the business sector has proved that we must have a single strong leader, a CEO (Chief Executive Officer), at the helm, and that the fast pace of today's world requires a robust organizational system that can react quickly to changes. Therefore, they insist, the church needs the imaginative and responsive leadership that methodical decision-making cannot deliver. They believe that the New Testament model is unrealistic for contemporary churches.

Those who dismiss the biblical design pose their apprehensions in such questions as: "If all elders are equal, then who leads the church?" "Doesn't this structure promote leaderless anarchy or stagnation?" "Doesn't the congregation need a single strong leader like a corporation?" "Don't we need someone with clear vision to lead us? The elders can't create a vision for the church."

There are two general answers to criticisms of the utility of the New Testament model (the leadership of the church by a council of elders). First, we must be guided by a concept amply illustrated in Scripture, that of primus inter pares, *first among equals*,[26] a key component of shared leadership. Second, the fact is that churches of all sizes have successfully implemented this model.

FIRST AMONG EQUALS

The principle of first among equals differentiates responsible biblical leadership—which is derived from calling and gifting—from the exercise of power over others by virtue of a select office. First among equals means that certain elders will distinguish themselves, by virtue of their gifts, abilities, and God's calling, in providing direction in an organization of equals *without* assuming a position of power over the other elders in the council. Such a responsibility is usually temporary and in terms of the body's current need, and is like the exercise of

42

leadership in the early church, at various times and to differing degrees of responsibility, by Peter, Paul, and James.

The concept of first among equals is perverted when used to justify a permanent, preeminent position for an individual (or individuals) at the expense of others who may be more gifted to lead under certain current circumstances. This is not always entirely the fault of the leader. Often congregations and boards will seek a "king" or endow their preachers with priestly status (1 Sam. 8:4–7).

First among equals differentiates responsible biblical leadership—which is derived from calling and gifting—from the exercise of power over others by virtue of a select office.

It is essential for the church to have strong, effective men initiating, organizing, providing oversight of its ministries, and leading the congregation. Admittedly, teams find it hard to create proposals, so, at the outset, some elder must initiate (or organize, or lead). The same precept is true for all other aspects of the council's leadership. Its exercise of leadership is expressed through individual elders "taking the lead" in a variety of venues and occasions, as the council delegates responsibility to the appropriately gifted individuals in their midst.

No one man has all the gifts necessary, and no one man has the time and energy to lead effectively all the activities of the church. In His providence, God calls individual men to have particular concerns for specialized aspects of His work in His church. Furthermore, for a season, He gives certain men exceptional determination and enables them to make great sacrifices of personal time to devote themselves to a particular effort.

In the church we often operate with a distorted view of leadership. True leadership is not dependent on robust egos or authoritarian behaviors. In fact, research on how accomplished, visionary leaders lead is startling: *All of the essential behaviors of a true leader are compatible with his also serving as an equal on a team.* Stephen Robbins lists these behaviors as:

- The process [of influencing followers] begins by the leader articulating an appealing vision. This vision provides a sense of continuity for followers by linking the present with a better future for the organization.

- The leader then communicates high performance expectations and expresses confidence that the followers can attain them. This enhances follower self-esteem and self-confidence.

- Next, the leader conveys, through words and actions, a new set of values and, by his . . . behavior, sets an example for followers to imitate.

- Finally, the leader makes self-sacrifices and engages in unconventional behavior to demonstrate courage and convictions about the vision. [27]

SUCCESSFUL IMPLEMENTATIONS

Most agree that collective elder leadership works well in small churches. However, I encounter a good bit of skepticism about the practicality of the New Testament model for larger churches that have grown beyond several hundred. The fact is, the model is effectively thriving in larger churches! Five outstanding examples are the Littleton Bible Chapel, Littleton, Colorado; the Peninsula Bible Churches (North and South) in Palo Alto and Cupertino, California; Grace Fellowship Church in Timonium, Maryland; and Church of the Saviour in Wayne, Pennsylvania. The last four have adult congregations of more than fifteen hundred. Most have successfully replicated their ministry models in their church plants. Each has extended the principle of the equality of elders into the pulpit. Their pulpits are filled by several elders, men who are gifted teachers and who serve as equals of the other elders on the churches' elder councils. While using a number of men to fill the pulpit is not essential to biblical governance, the practice certainly reinforces its values.

TEAMWORK IN THE PULPIT

Teamwork in the pulpit—with coordinated preaching—can be more effective than the senior pastor's undertaking all the preaching. Coordinated preaching means that the sermons are related week-to-week, either by topical theme or an expository series, and each preacher leads the congregation in the same direction. Comprehension and motivation are reinforced by multiple viewpoints and personalities. In this way, the people are taught by men with a diversity of gifts, each reinforcing the work of the others. A shared

44

pulpit models teamwork, respect for others' various gifts, and a corporate, not an individual, purpose. Each man on the team demonstrates that the benefit of the preachers' combined diversity of gifts to the congregation is more significant to him than his personal renown. Best of all, the focus is shifted from the preacher to the content, to hearing from God. People invite their friends to attend the church to benefit from a series on Men of Faith, Godly Parenting, Marriage, Genesis, or Romans, not to hear "our great preacher."

A shared pulpit models teamwork, respect for others' gifts, and a corporate, not an individual, purpose.

The team approach has additional benefits. The focus on just one family in the church, the senior pastor's—and the unintended consequence of loss of privacy for all members of that household—is greatly reduced. Also, the departure of one preaching team member may be handled without the crisis that usually accompanies the resignation of a senior pastor. The process of replacing one member of a team can be achieved with minimal disruption. One of the greatest benefits is that each preacher is freed from preparing a sermon each week. He can then be visibly providing active leadership as an elder in his areas of gifting.

Church of the Saviour, with an attendance of two thousand, has successfully used coordinated team preaching by three men. This format enables each man to focus on a particular aspect of ministry as well as sermon preparation. In addition, this arrangement simultaneously allowed the church to support the preaching at a church plant for its initial year.

However, the shared pulpit requires care in its implementation. Coordinated preaching gives the church a stable expectation from week to week. Failure to coordinate may deny the congregation many of the benefits mentioned above and the spiritual needs of the body may well not be addressed. The principle of elder governance should not be contradicted in practice: elder governance must include determining the subjects that are preached and taught in the church, thereby properly feeding and protecting the flock. Consequently, the elders should give direction to those who have this preaching and teaching responsibility. The decision on what is preached in the church should come from the elders' prayerful, collective judgment, driven by the needs of the body. If an individual elder is persuaded by the Holy Spirit to address a particular need, he certainly ought to be able to convince the other elders.

Those who share in the preaching need to be careful to honor the diversity of each other's gifts, and to permit and encourage each other's freedom of expression. Away from the pulpit, the preaching team must avoid acting as a two-, three-, or four-headed senior pastor by isolating themselves from the other elders or assuming a collective, superior position. Furthermore, this state of affairs can be aggravated if these men insist on seeking the concurrence of *each other* on leadership decisions instead of the advice of the *full* body of elders. This elitism may look like subservience to one another, but it is not proper elder behavior because it is not deference to all the elders. The conditions for teamwork between preachers and the total elder council are promoted by team preaching, but unless the entire process is carried out with humility and purpose, the shared pulpit does not assure such teamwork.

TENTMAKERS AS EQUAL PARTNERS

People who doubt the practicality of the New Testament model also object that tentmaking elders can never be equal partners in churches that employ full-time, paid staff members. Besides assuming such elders will not make the necessary sacrifices from their families, careers, and recreation to lead ministries, they claim that since these men are not physically based at the church office (their work is not done on site), they cannot keep in touch with their ministries. Those who argue this way cite personal experience with elders' reluctance to take on responsibility, or their unavailability at the "necessary" moment. However, from what I have seen, the same complaint is made about most "full-time" church staff. "Just when you need them, they are off at some conference."

The allegation that part-time, tentmaking elders are unable to hold their own with full-time paid staff is not based on an accurate observation of the biblical model at work. Anyone who has worked with a church plant, or a small church, knows that busy men will contribute prodigious amounts of time and energy to ministry. Many examples could be given of tentmaking elders taking charge of important ministries and shepherding those in their charge when they are allowed to be *equal* partners on a ministry team. These are bivocational men who do not let their secular careers take over their lives, thereby freeing themselves for opportunities for significant service. True, this kind of elder service only flourishes if the leadership of the church establishes a climate conducive to the proper recognition of such gifted servants, but it is possible and does occur.

The belief that ministry leaders must be co-located is a holdover from before computers and the internet when society was locked into a fixed work week and workplace. This conviction is overturned by the advancement of technological communication. Industry has appropriated the benefits of telecommuting, flextime, and part-time employees. This revolution in the use of personnel has been made possible by the advent and use of cellphones, teleconferencing, and the internet. There is no reason why the church should resist adopting these technical means, and no reason why a ministry leader must be in the same building or on the same schedule as paid staff. In reality, most meetings of ministry support teams take place in the evenings and on weekends, outside the normal church office work week.

WHAT IS THE REAL IMPEDIMENT?

In his discussion of team leadership, George Barna laments:

> Despite the obvious advantages, for thousands of pastors such a transition [to team leadership] is impossible. They were raised to believe that the pastor leads everyone and must have direct, unfettered oversight of the masses. . . .
>
> Perhaps we can adapt an old axiom and posit that it takes a mature leader to embrace team leadership, because it demands giving up the spotlight, the authority, and the view of the pastor as the center of all church activity.[28]

It is the environment we have created, allowed to grow, and continue to feed that sabotages dedicated elders' involvement in the church. The "successful" church, with its paid staff and its congregation of spectators—and the resulting mindset—defeats volunteer leadership.

It is the environment we have created, allowed to grow, and continue to feed that sabotages dedicated elders' involvement in the church.

The formation of the value of a life of service is not likely to take place in this climate of consumerism. In a small church or church plant, men take on large responsibilities and have the commensurate authority to lead in those areas. As a result, ownership and a sense of accomplishment flourish. Conversely, in many larger churches, the professional staff assumes the up-front leadership of the ministries and directs the volunteers to do the behind-the-scenes support work under their supervision. After all, in many cases, the staff was trained in seminaries to consider church management their responsibility. Amazingly, this way of thinking prevails although they received almost no instruction there in how to manage people (unlike many people in their churches).

Though their instinct is that elders' efforts are not on a par with their own, the staff bemoans the fact that men will not make a substantial commitment of time to ministry. Is this not ignoring the truth that men in general—and certainly men of elder quality—are not going to sacrifice a portion of their active lives to be involved in inconsequential matters in which their participation is not crucial to the outcome? Men will work extremely hard if the task is significant in God's economy. In interviews, elders say that, in their church's initial years when they were part of the ministry team, they felt like real biblical elders. But now that their churches have grown and all the ministries are headed by professionals, they have the impression they are nonessential players. Their creative initiatives are often judged to be rogue behavior or an attempt to usurp someone's power and invade his turf. This is tragic.

The Holy Spirit has made you overseers.
Acts 20:28

Chapter 3

The Elder

A S THE ELDER COUNCIL'S SUCCESS IN GOVERNING depends on the quality of its members, we must look carefully at how men are added to their number. Just as was urged upon Timothy and Titus, those currently leading must exercise great wisdom in the appropriate selection of elders. We will now consider how we carry out this responsibility.

APPOINTMENT OF ELDERS

Who selects elders? How is each man appointed and for how long? How does he relate to other leadership? What is the congregation's role? The stands taken on these major issues—and the practical execution of the church's policies—will determine the biblical character of the elder council. I think we will see that Scripture's teaching, its examples and directives, may point in a direction that is quite different from most evangelical church practice.

It is the Holy Spirit who appoints elders.

However, no matter how we settle the question of who recognizes men to be elders and how, we need to bear in mind that Scripture is explicit in stating that it is the Holy Spirit who makes the appointment: "The Holy Spirit has made you overseers, to shepherd the church of God" (Acts 20:28). Therefore, in choosing a method of elder selection, we must acknowledge that we cannot and should not *create* elders. We are merely identifying those whom the Holy Spirit has previously appointed.

THE ELDER

NEW TESTAMENT BACKGROUND

The New Testament record shows that God provided a variety of servants to address the needs of the new congregations of the early church. These servants functioned as apostles, prophets, evangelists, teachers, shepherds, teachers, workers of miracles, healers, administrators, and translators (1 Thess. 5:12–13; 1 Cor. 12:27–30; Eph. 4:11–12). The apostles themselves, and other elders under their instruction, selected some of these workers to be elders. How did they recognize those the Holy Spirit had appointed?

The incumbent leaders chose those men who aspired to serve, were morally qualified, and had demonstrated the leadership ability expected of an elder. Above all, they examined the evidence of the candidates' calling: "These men must also first be tested" (in 1 Tim. 3:10, the "also" connects "these men" with the elder candidates previously mentioned). Therefore, all New Testament elders were involved in ministry leadership, *but* not all ministry workers were elders. Elders were a subset of the shepherds in the church: those men who exhibited the qualifications of 1 Timothy 3 and Titus 1, and had acted upon the Holy Spirit's calling to be shepherd-leaders.

If we adhere to the New Testament method in our churches, elders will be appointed only by *other currently, fully qualified elders*. As Paul explained to Titus, "For this reason I left you in Crete, that you would set in order what remains and appoint elders in every city as I directed you" (Titus 1:5). The congregations did not elect elders in the New Testament period: Paul and Barnabas "appointed elders for them in every church, [and] having prayed with fasting, they commended them to the Lord in whom they had believed" (Acts 14:23). This was not accidental, but in accordance with the apostolic order, "as I directed you" (Titus 1:5). Those elders selected by the apostles, in turn, appointed other qualified men as elders—again, as they had been commanded: "Entrust these [the things which you have been taught] to faithful [reliable] men who will be able to teach others also" (2 Tim. 2:2).

LIMITATIONS ON THE ROLE OF THE CONGREGATION

Now the question is, how does the example of New Testament practice translate into our present situation? My view is that the biblical model prohibits the election of elders by the congregation. Reasons for this conclusion are:

- The elder is not an elected representative of the congregation. He is that man who has been recognized by other elders as having been appointed by the Holy Spirit to

50

shepherd the flock of His church: "The Holy Spirit has made you overseers, to shepherd the church of God" (Acts 20:28).

- An individual congregant (who is not an elder) cannot be expected to pass authoritative judgment on whether the qualifications of the elder appointee under consideration are sufficient—that is, whether he meets the high standards set forth in Scripture. Requiring church members to do so is equivalent to asking the community of his patients to certify their medical specialist, instead of insisting that he is board-certified by his peers.

- The individual congregant does not possess and cannot obtain sufficient firsthand knowledge of *each and all* of the elder candidates to be added to the council. The qualifications for eldership are so extensive and stringent, that facts on each man must be gathered by a careful process: "Do not lay hands upon anyone too hastily and thereby share responsibility for the sins of others; keep yourself free from sin" (1 Tim. 5:22).

- If the congregation elects elders, it is not held accountable, individually or corporately, for its decisions, because, in the normal format of a congregational meeting, the individual voters do not have to explain the rationale for their decisions. But, Scripture teaches it is the elders "who will [be required to] give an account" (Heb. 13:17).

- If congregations elect elders, there exists the possibility of rule by a small minority of people. In a church that has a twenty-five percent quorum requirement (in order to do business at congregational meetings), a matter can be decided by as little as thirteen percent of the congregation. If the stated percentage required to approve an elder is raised above a simple majority, the situation is even worse. In the case of a two-thirds vote of ratification, a mere nine percent of the congregation can determine who serves as elders. This means that anywhere between nine and thirteen percent of the members of a church have the power to unseat an elder (governance by minority).

- Churches that practice congregational voting to affirm the elder council may put women in the position of exercising authority over men: "But I do not allow a woman to teach or *exercise authority* over a man" (1 Tim. 2:12, italics added). Even among complementarian scholars, opinion is divided on whether a woman's participation in a church corporate decision is an exercise of authority.[*] However, if we believe that elders exercise authority through the corporate decisions of the council, then it follows that the same thing occurs when a woman participates in a congregational corporate action, the affirmation of elders. This being true, this practice actually makes the church responsible (through its bylaws) for requiring women members to be in authority over men and to take action actually forbidden in Scripture. Corporate decisions on budgets, building programs, ministry initiatives, and the like do not entail the problem of involving women in the decision to seat or unseat elders.

NECESSARY ROLE OF THE CONGREGATION

The New Testament-instituted practice of appointment of elders by elders clarifies the proper role of the members of the church. Although the congregation is not equipped to approve elders, it should maintain a good measure of influence. It has the privilege and duty of encouraging and supporting potential elder candidates, and of bringing to the attention of current council elders the qualifications and service of these men.

How does the congregation play its vital role in the selection of elders? First, members of the congregation should be routinely identifying men they observe becoming biblically qualified as elders, encouraging them, and "appreciat[ing] those who diligently labor among you" (1 Thess. 5:12). Appointment to eldership should be the result of a long process that started when younger men were encouraged to take on increasingly more responsible leadership roles

---

[*] John Piper and Wayne Grudem write: "The reason we do not think this [women voting in a congregational meeting] is inconsistent with 1 Timothy 2:12 is that the authority of the church is not the same as the authority of the individuals who make up the church. When we say the congregation has authority, we do not mean that each man and each woman has that authority. Therefore, gender, as a part of individual personhood, is not significantly in view in corporate congregational decisions."[29]

in the church. Christian brothers and sisters perform an important service whenever they recognize the potential in a man to be a godly leader, and paint a vision for him of how God could use him. We all gratefully remember those who encouraged us and invested the effort and energy to mentor us.

Members of the congregation should be routinely identifying men they observe becoming biblically qualified as elders.

Second, the congregation is obligated to bring to the elder council's attention, before the actual appointment of any new elder, any facts supporting this action or proving that the man is not qualified. This can be facilitated by announcing to the body, well in advance of any final action by the council, the names of those men under the council's consideration, those men who are personally considering their own willingness to serve. Simultaneously, the council should solicit the church members' comments, with the understanding that it is obligated to investigate and determine the truth of anything so offered. This guarantees that the council's decision either to affirm or disqualify the man is based on all available information.

Participation of the congregation in this way empowers the individual member in the appointment of elders far more than would his ballot in a congregational vote. In the latter, the member's influence is merely his one vote. His only other way of having an effect on the outcome is to be involved in an unseemly floor debate (in the congregational meeting) on the qualifications (excellent or poor) of a candidate, a situation that provides no opportunity for anyone to investigate the truthfulness of his statements. However, by bringing information to the council while it is considering candidates, the member is assured that the council will carefully investigate his testimony and he will have a major influence on the outcome. Also, a woman may bring a concern about, or an affirmation of, a prospective elder to the council for their investigation. But this is not exercising authority over the man, which would be the case were she voting to bar him from the council.

Third, besides witnessing the new elders being commissioned by the incumbent elders, through the laying on of hands and prayer, a beneficial step for the people of the church to take is a formal commitment to support the newly appointed elders in their service on the council. Incorporating this act as part of a congregational gathering (annual or other meeting) stands as a reminder that all members are under the biblical obligation of submitting to the authority of the eldership and supporting them in prayer. At this point, we need to be careful that a vote of affirmation has not become in reality a vote to confirm an elder or elders. The test is simple: if the vote can affect the outcome, then we have simply disguised voting by calling it "affirming." The congregation's commitment should be expressed just like the question and response in a wedding ceremony when the congregation is asked to support the marriage.

These congregational responsibilities and privileges should be understood as the members' substantial role in the life and governance of the church. The leadership ought to establish and promote an atmosphere of commitment to leadership development and multiplication, and not just in terms of current needs. They should both model it and teach the congregation how it is done. Crucial to God's work in the world is the continual replication of elders, for such men are the sine qua non of our churches and church planting, locally and internationally.

THE COUNCIL'S ROLE

There is no more serious and critical task for the eldership than the appointment of men to the council. The incumbent elders must identify and select those men that the Lord has already called to the office. Their previous appointment by the Holy Spirit will have been made evident through their current ministry leadership in the local church, their standing with those they are serving, and their sense of calling. Moreover, and of equal significance, a qualified man is to be selected whether or not he represents a particular viewpoint. While it is vital that elders be men who are well versed in knowledge of Scripture, able to make and carefully articulate determined biblical judgments, a man should never be denied recognition as elder out of partisan considerations. For instance, the expectation that he may be outspoken or is known to have reservations about a particular initiative is never grounds for denying eldership. However, the man's willingness and ability to support consensus are crucial biblical requirements for serving on the council: He may not be "pugnacious" (Titus 1:7), and he must be "self-controlled" (Titus 1:8), and "peaceable" (1 Tim. 3:3).[30]

Also, a man should not be placed on the council primarily because he supports a faction within the leadership, though this is contrary to prevalent advice coming from some senior pastors. The later advise their compatriots to involve themselves in the elder selection process to achieve a council that will support their philosophy of ministry.[31] However, the standards of elder equivalence and plurality make it absolutely necessary that a group of men whose loyalty is to Christ, not to another leader within the church, is in place.

By way of preparation and consensus building, men who are being seriously considered for selection as elders should first complete a course on the role of the elders,[*] and the history, theology, purpose, vision, policies, and procedures of the church. In this context, each candidate ought to be prayerfully considering his calling. The men and their wives should be interviewed to find out if they are willing to commit the time and effort to fulfill the responsibilities of the position and have their families' support. Only when all these aspects of the process are finished may the council consider the men's appointment.

LACK OF CANDIDATES

Many authorities on creating strong, collaborative leadership teams stress recruiting the best talent possible, and it is true that great groups or teams are composed of great individuals.[32] Still, the church cannot create elders. To appoint men to eldership because they are outstanding leaders elsewhere is unbiblical and foolhardy. Instead, we must appoint men whom the Holy Spirit has already appointed, who have demonstrated that appointment through their visible service in the church.

Men will not labor as true elders unless the church is organized in such a way that volunteer service is *essential* for the body to function.

All that has been said here about the appointment of elders is predicated on this proviso: Men are already undertaking the work and role of elders among God's people. But here we must face the undeniable truth—and face it squarely—that men will not labor as true elders unless the church is organized in such a way that such

---

[*] I recommend Alexander Strauch, *The Study Guide to Biblical Eldership*, and Alexander Strauch and Richard Swartley, *The Mentor's Guide to Biblical Eldership*, supplemented by the church's own statements of doctrine, values, vision, positions, and policies.

volunteer service is *essential* for the body to function. If all the leadership of the church is the responsibility of staff and vocational elders, no room remains for other equipped men to serve in leadership. No setting exists, no occasion occurs, for them to sense God's calling them to eldership. No opportunity arises for incumbent leadership to observe those whom God is calling.

As mentioned previously, this is not a problem in start-up churches where everyone must pitch in so that the mission of the new endeavor will succeed, and enthusiasm is high. However, this Gordian knot (both of our own making *and* unbiblical) becomes a severe challenge in established churches where staff has been hired to fill all the key positions and the congregation has become passive.

Elders Must Be Called

It does not matter that it is difficult to secure enough elders for godly biblical leadership: It is God's method. Elders must receive a call to service from the Holy Spirit: Each "aspires to the office" (1 Tim. 3:1), is appointed by the Holy Spirit (Acts 20:28), and serves voluntarily, according to the will of God (1 Peter 5:2). An elder's appointment to the elder council by other elders is an acknowledgment that the divine appointment has already occurred. How does this process unfold?

A review of the manner in which both missionaries and preachers choose their career paths throws light on the question of how the elder's calling takes place (from the perspective of those watching). In the case of those headed for a vocation in missions, they have attended missions conferences where men and women have been challenged to dedicate their lives to God's plan for the world. They have heard sermons on the Great Commission and their responsibility to pick up the task. They have seen this lifework honored from the pulpit and have befriended missionaries who described their calling and commitment. As a result, these Christians have been able to visualize the possibility of their own similar contribution to the kingdom, and are open to the Holy Spirit as He leads them to commit their lives to the training, lifelong endeavors, and sacrifices required of missionaries.

The situation is similar for those men who prepare for service as preachers. They have observed men pouring their lives into the flock—preaching, leading, and counseling. If they have similar gifts, men can envision themselves in that role. Because of this visualization and their divinely implanted desire to serve the Lord, the Holy Spirit gives them the calling to obtain specialized preparation for a lifelong career in the ministry.

In short, the church has a strategic part to play in developing workers for the harvest. If the church made no provision for prospective missionaries or pastoral candidates to envision and consider their future service, how many would sense the calling?

But why on earth would any man be drawn to decide to make the sacrifices from his career, family, and recreation to become *a bivocational, tentmaking elder*? In most churches, none of the influences mentioned above that led to "full-time service" for preachers and missionaries are in effect for potential elders. No conferences are held in the church encouraging such dedicated work. Sermons do not uphold the value of eldership, much less champion it. Elder service is not envisioned for young men as the outcome of steps of increasing responsibility. The elders' service in the church is largely administrative, taking place in meetings behind closed doors, or it passes unmentioned, uncredited, not counted. And every time a preacher refers to himself as "pastor," in distinction from "the elders," he further depreciates the role of the elder, including his own position as elder. One observation here. The tragic result of our negligence (and the way the elder function is often viewed), is that the wrong men, those who aspire to power and control rather than ministry, are drawn to eldership.

Why on earth would any man be drawn to decide to make the sacrifices from his career, family, and recreation to become *a bivocational, tentmaking elder*?

It is simply unlikely that a person will select a career in missionary service if he matures in a church that does not support missions. How many young men commit themselves to the lengthy and arduous process of preparation for the pastoral ministry who were never personally challenged to do so by another brother? Then why would we expect men to hear, much less heed, a calling to true biblical eldership in churches that neither herald the value of elder ministry leadership, nor have ministries that are dependent on elders' participation and direction?

Elders are called to God's service in the same way missionaries and shepherd-teachers are, by observing the service of other men at work and being encouraged to consider the possibility of joining them. When men *see* and *hear* of elders working in the body, the Holy Spirit nurtures them in recognizing both the need and their own desire to employ their gifts. They are able to visualize filling that role. They step forward in response to His call, prepare themselves to serve, and begin to lead. They come to consider their secular careers valuable means of supporting their ministries, not all-consuming ends unto themselves. Those men who so "aspire" should be afforded specialized training, and, once qualified and sufficiently seasoned through a considerable period of service, they should be recognized as elders by the church and entrusted with more responsibility.

Our understanding of God at work should energize our support of the value of elder leadership. But, if the church does not provide the atmosphere for such development and the context for true elder service, there will be a dearth of worthy men who sense the opportunity, imagine themselves serving, and, consequently, aspire to be elders.

Over-Dependence on Staff

As churches grow, they often add staff to handle office and ministry logistics. Although this may be prudent, once a church departs from an all volunteer structure, it runs the risk of turning a participatory congregation into one that is passive and dependent on staff. The chief reason larger churches become overly dependent on paid staff is readily understood: as soon as one person is a paid employee, he begins to think it easier to manage an all paid staff than a mixed staff-and-volunteer organization. With paid staff, the leverage of employment, salary, and working environment provide the incentives. With volunteers, staff and elders must invest time and effort in their recognition, mentoring, encouragement, and motivation. Admittedly, because of their outside employment, bivocational tentmakers can only handle about one-third of the responsibility of a full-time employee, and a mixed leadership team will be larger than an all-staff-led management team. Whether or not it is more unwieldy and less efficient is a matter of how the team is organized. Most big families would also be easier to manage if they had fewer members.

**Right here—just at this point—
biblical governance succeeds or fails**

Right here—just at this point—biblical governance succeeds or fails. Many acknowledge the biblical pattern espoused here, but in practice revert to a staff-led church out of frustration over not having enough elder candidates willing to fulfill their biblical responsibilities. Consequently, they default to a format in which their elders serve only as a board of directors.

Some senior pastors even argue that it is impossible to find qualified men, and even advocate bringing unqualified men onto a board and providing on-the-job training.[33] But, these same pastors also express the fear that men who do not support the pastors' philosophy of ministry will be put on the board, and will, in fact, destroy the board's ability to operate. To head off this result, the pastor makes himself the gatekeeper in the candidate consideration process, and, at the same time, hides this confiscated role under cover of the confidentiality of the nominating procedure.[34]

Such conduct and conditions have visited on us our present dilemma, a dearth of available and willing leadership. George Barna points out:

> Our research has shown that within the past couple of years the Christian Church has driven away literally more than one million Christians who are gifted leaders. Many of them departed simply because they could not stand being at a church that had ineffective leadership. Others left because in thousands and thousands of churches a true leader is a threat to the pastor (who, in those cases, is not truly a leader) and is intentionally kept away from leadership duties. . . . Those [threatened] pastors often assume that the presence of effective lay leaders will inevitably tarnish the pastor's image and job security, placing their livelihood and their platform to do what they enjoy doing (for example, preaching) in jeopardy.[35]

Conducive Environment

Despite the difficulties, if a church desires to be biblically led by true elders, it must maintain the leadership environment in which these potential elders can thrive. Ample challenges and opportunities for motivated men to serve in areas of increasing responsibility and leadership (as they mature in the Lord) must be provided. If this milieu exists, men who have proved their elder calling through ministry leadership will become available to serve on the council. The risk of appointing men to the council who will not support the philosophy of ministry of the church is eliminated if the men selected have already displayed their ability to serve within that ministry framework. We do not have to adopt unbiblical selection approaches if our churches provide the appropriate fertile fields for the development of elders.

THE ELDER

One of the most logical, entry-level opportunities for service is already in place in many churches, the leadership of a small fellowship and Bible study. This role combines the leadership, shepherding, teaching, and discipling of a microcongregation. For the aspiring elder, shepherding such a small group offers an excellent proving ground of his qualifications, and also for his consideration of God's calling to additional future responsibilities.

The Bible study also provides such a maturing leader the venue for exercising his teaching ability in a style that is different from preaching. Many men are discouraged from teaching because they define it in terms of the presentation method modeled in the pulpit. A man who does not have the gifting to preach in front of hundreds may be very effective in a seminar format or inductive approach. By the way, the effectiveness of his teaching should be judged by the outcome in the lives of its recipients. If the truth be told, retention of biblical knowledge and its application to life by the participants in a small group inductive Bible study is much greater than that of those who passively listen to a sermon.

If tentmaking and vocational elders will assume the responsibility of developing apprentices as leaders, men can be matured for any role in the church.

Shepherding small groups is not the only place of service for potential elders. Any area of ministry can be a venue for tentmakers, even filling the pulpit. Bear in mind that God gave us our existing leadership to employ various means (gifts) "for the equipping of the saints for the work of service, to the building up of the body of Christ; until we all attain to the unity of the faith, and of the knowledge of the Son of God, to a mature man, to the measure of the stature which belongs to the fullness of Christ" (Eph. 4:12–13). If tentmaking and vocational elders will assume the responsibility of developing apprentices as leaders, men can be matured for any role in the church. We have Paul's example before us. The apostle usually took with him a peer *and* an apprentice. And the New Testament shows us how the apostles devoted themselves to training the first elders. Answering the general call for the church to be in the disciple-making business is a specific elder obligation. If true elders are to be developed in the church, each incumbent elder must resist the temptation to carry out his responsibilities alone. Instead, as often as possible, he will involve a potentially emerging elder to assist him in his tasks.

THE ELDER

Of special note are the creative men. They are often lost to eldership for several reasons. First, such a man may lack the corresponding administrative skills to accomplish his vision alone, and, if not involved in a team, he will become frustrated. Second, we are much more receptive to the person with administrative or managerial skills who will help us implement *our* vision than we are to a man who brings a new vision. Such creative men must be encouraged and supported as they mature if they are to become elders eventually. It has grieved me to see stellar talent lost to the leadership of the church because the unusual gifting of these servants was not honored and cultivated.

Inadequate Solutions

Some so-called elder recruitment is actually arm-twisting, but this is not the solution to a lack of candidates. We are tempted to feel in desperate need, especially when searching for a particular expertise, as in a treasurer. However, Peter says elders are to "shepherd the flock, . . . not under compulsion, but voluntarily, according to the will of God, . . . with eagerness" (1 Peter 5:2). Abilities and gifting are important. However, the calling and character qualifications of the elder must always take precedence. If we compromise here, the church will pay the consequences.

Inherently, we create our own hazards if we de facto decide that the realm of bivocational leadership will be exclusively, or primarily, the administrative tasks of the church, such as finance, facilities, long-range planning, personnel management, and so forth, while the ministries of the church are reserved for the hired staff. We slide into this easily because many men bring the required skills for these assignments from their secular careers. Though these jobs need to be filled, they do not require elders, men with the special gifting and calling of shepherds and teachers. Using men who are gifted in teaching and shepherding in nothing more than administrative duties robs the church of their potential service as elders.

STAFF ELDERS

Most large, elder-led churches have both vocational and bivocational elders. The use of the word or title "pastor" to designate a paid-staff or vocational elder is not helpful, and, as has been previously asserted, there is no New Testament position or office of "pastor." Pastoring is the *function of shepherding*, that is, caring for the flock.

THE ELDER

The word literally means the work of sheepherding, and the term for "flock" comes from the same word.

It is imperative that the congregation is frequently reminded that the only distinction biblically between a staff elder who serves as a preacher, and a tentmaking elder is in terms of their gifting. Many churches sensitive to this issue have dropped what has become the position title of "pastor," and use the term "elder" to refer to all elders. Preachers who are elders should always refer to themselves or any other elder as a "fellow elder," following the examples of Peter (1 Peter 5:1) and John (2 John 1, 3 John 1); and all elders are wise to model elder equivalence. Leaders should never allow the words they use to convey a *we-them* attitude.

Leaders should never allow the words they use to convey a *we-them* attitude.

A biblical elder council will be composed of some who serve the church part time and some who are full time. Because of this, some argue that the authority of the individual elders should be in proportion to how much time they dedicate to church work. According to this thinking, the leadership of the church really emanates primarily from the paid-staff elders. However, examination of the example of the Jerusalem conference recorded in Acts 15 does not reveal any evidence of some men asserting authority over others. To the contrary, even the apostles who were present did not claim or act on their apostolic authority, but demonstrated their commitment to the importance of obtaining a decision by consensus of the elders.

Salaried staff fulfill designated areas of responsibility and perform assigned duties under the direction of the council. However, because a man has been hired for a particular position "on staff," including the job of preacher, he does not receive the automatic right to govern the church or to be part of the elder council. Jesus warns about the potential for divided loyalty: "He who is a hired hand, and not a shepherd, who is not the owner of the sheep, sees the wolf coming, and leaves the sheep and flees. . . . He flees because he is a hired hand and is not concerned about the sheep" (John 10:12–13). No one wants to be called a "hireling," and we never refer to staff members as "hirelings," but good manners should not blind us to heeding our Lord's warning on split allegiance. For example, if a member of the paid staff is to be appointed an elder, it must first be established that his loyalty is to the Chief Shepherd and to the church he is serving, rather than to his career. This is a daunting task, one that must be undertaken with the greatest seriousness. Further, to avoid conflict of interest, a man on staff who is also an elder must recuse himself from any decision that affects his employment, and he cannot be involved in the review and evaluation of his own position.

There is another aspect of adding elders to the existing council's ranks. For how long? And, in the case of a good-sized council, how is the term of office handled?

TERM LIMITS

Are term limits for elders a good idea? No evidence of such appears in the New Testament, and mention of this concept is noticeably lacking in the directions stating the requirements for the office of elder. And there are other uncertainties: What if a man needs to resign from the council? How is he to be regarded after that and how do we refer to him?

> **Mandatory rotation for elders is no more biblical than it would be for missionaries, preachers, and evangelists.**

It is my belief that an elder should continue to serve as long as he continues to meet the biblical qualifications and perseveres in fulfilling the duties of the office. But many churches are in the habit of periodically making God's servants, often their church's most gifted servants, step down from the council! Mandatory rotation for elders is no more biblical than it would be for missionaries, preachers, and evangelists. Time off for rest, emphasis on a particular ministry, family needs, or emergencies are occasions for a sabbatical, not removal from the elder council. Those who argue for mandatory rotation of elders might as well be consistent and insist upon finite terms for those filling the pulpit of the church, after which they are required to seek other employment.

"NEW BLOOD"

Some will advocate that restrictions on the length of time elders serve is imperative to prevent the council's becoming set in its ways. When eldership is viewed as a position of power, such an attitude is understandable. But if ongoing accountability for meeting the scriptural criteria for office is maintained, council elders will not become entrenched or abusive of power. Besides the unbiblical precedent of setting term limits, the approach of introducing untested, immature men, supposedly in order to refresh leadership, is not a biblical remedy. A godly, mature council will always be generating and considering new ideas, originating from inside and outside its ranks, and will persevere in its responsibility to disciple the next generation of leaders. Replication of available qualified men should lead to church growth through new ministries and church planting.

ROTATION

The practice of annually rotating off a significant portion of the council, often as much as one-third, is very disruptive of council cohesion and effectiveness. It takes years for a man to become a fully effective team player (in the elder council context), learning how to work well together with the others and within the constraints upon them. Also to be mastered is an informed understanding of the path the church has traveled in advancing to its present ministry plan. Under a replacement system, just when a man becomes fully productive, he is removed from maximum usefulness.

Changes such as employment or relocation will introduce unavoidable alterations in the council. But to impose a policy of rotation as well will only weaken the council's ability to serve the church consistently. Rotation of elders also seriously exacerbates the depreciation of tent-making elders by staff elders. The employed staff remain permanently in their leadership positions, whether or not they are serving on the council, which is not true of those tent-making elders being asked to step aside for an interval.

Rotation of key volunteer leaders will always result in the bureaucracy (or staff) taking over.

I observed an analogous situation while working in the aerospace industry and interfacing with various government agencies, some of which were directed by military officers, supported by a civilian staff. In this case, as they progressed in their careers, the military officers were rotated in and out of a particular organization. Because they were short timers in these assignments, the agency's permanent staff, while not in charge and not tasked to make decisions, was able to control the organization bureaucratically. Understandably, this awkward style correlated with the lack of success of these groups, since, in stark contrast, those agencies with permanent staffs of managers and support personnel were able to consistently outperform their counterparts. This evaluation is shared and freely confessed by both business analysts and Congressional oversight committees. Rotation of key volunteer leaders will always result in the bureaucracy (or staff) taking over.

Another argument proffered for limiting the elder's term is the thought that this is the only practical way to replace an unproductive elder. I have personally experienced the pain involved in the necessary step of removing men from the elder council. I know how difficult it is. However, allowing an unqualified elder to stay in place until rotation removes him is wrong. To do so is to act without biblical precedence. Moreover, we penalize the church if we put in place a system that withdraws the services of godly elders in order (on the rare occasions when this occurs) to be able to remove unproductive ones.

On the other hand, since we always need to guard against servant roles turning into positions of power, setting term limits on holding the office of moderator within the council is prudent. By this method, the moderator is changed at some designated interval. Besides preventing the moderator of the council from becoming entrenched in his position, this policy provides for the equipping of more men.

Many organizations employ the wise technique of the orderly succession from the office of vice-moderator to that of moderator in order to train the moderator-to-be adequately before he takes on his duties. For instance, every two, three, or four years, the council elects a new vice-moderator, and the incumbent vice-moderator becomes the moderator, the present moderator retiring from this position.

If the church treasurer is involved in setting financial policy, he should be one of the elders. In this case, because of the technical nature of the treasurer's task, progression from another position is not constructive. However, if the treasurer is assisted by another elder, that man will be prepared to undertake that responsibility later. Filling the secretary's job depends chiefly on ability or the willingness to handle the council's records and correspondence. All of this advice on succession is based on my years of experience and is not mandated by Scripture. This is also true of the remaining issues regarding term of service.

TITLE OF EMERITUS

What about the matter of elders who continue to be fully qualified in character and are active in ministry in the congregation, but who, by their own choice, currently prefer not to be involved in the leadership of the church? Should such elders be retained on the council? Since governing or overseeing is an integral part of the duty of an elder, the answer has to be no. A man who does not have the calling to oversee the church does not aspire to be or qualify as an elder. Shepherding alone does not make one an elder. In a healthy body, many people will be involved in shepherding and serving, including the women who are biblically excluded from eldership.

Moreover, the definition of elder should not be diluted by using the term as an honorary title for any man who is active in ministry. This weakening of the concept of elder is avoided when a practical way is found to distinguish between those currently serving and those who served in the past.

What is the most graceful way to handle the case of an elder who is no longer functioning as an elder? Many churches have found it appropriate to use the respectful designation *elder emeritus* to refer to that man who has resigned as elder because he is no longer able by virtue of age, health, or unavoidable commitments, to fulfill his elder obligations. He has become an elder emeritus, just as a retired pastor becomes a pastor emeritus. The use of the term emeritus should not be viewed as creating a new position in the church, since "emeritus" refers to a person no longer holding a position. Such men no longer have governing responsibility or authority. If the circumstances preventing such a man from serving change, he may again be restored to the office of elder. However, lack of desire to continue serving or the wish to give higher priority to his career should not result in a man's being given the elder emeritus designation.

Extensive wisdom and judgment reside in those who have experienced the course of a church's history and have weathered its missteps and hard times over the years. Failure to tap the benefit of the light these men shed on contemporary issues and their wise counsel is a besetting omission made by younger elders. Prudence dictates calling upon the wise elder emeritus for insight and advice, or for his service on an ad hoc committee.

The council's success in governing depends on the quality of the men. And this is enhanced by clear and purposeful practices in the areas of appointment and term duration. But what about how these men work with each other? How do they stay on the "the straight and narrow"?

RELATIONSHIPS

The quality of the relationships of the elders to each other, the staff, and the congregation is a major determinant and indicator of the biblical character of a church. Elders' character qualities are most apparent to the body when displayed in members' one-on-one interactions with each man. The congregation's overall opinion of, and confidence in, the elder council will be shaped by these individual assessments. To lead and govern effectively, elders' lives, both within and outside the elder council, must be exemplary. Elders are answerable to their brother elders, a chief application of the "one another" passages of Scripture.

ACCOUNTABILITY

Included in the elder's responsibilities is the charge to be continuously accountable. Each elder must frequently reexamine his own biblical qualification, and be evaluated regularly by his peer elders on the council. In Paul's farewell to the Ephesian elders, his counsel on self-evaluation and peer accountability is urgent and thought-provoking:

> Be on guard for *yourselves* and for all the flock, among which the Holy Spirit has made you overseers, to shepherd the church of God which He purchased with His own blood. I know that after my departure savage wolves will come in among you, not sparing the flock; and *from among your own selves* men will arise, speaking perverse things, to draw away the disciples after them. *Therefore be on the alert,* remembering that night and day for a period of three years I did not cease to admonish each one with tears (Acts 20:28–31; italics added).

We should not be repulsed by this passage, or avoid applying it simply because it mentions the extreme situation of an elder or elders ("savage wolves") attempting to split the church. Although this situation seems unimaginable to most, it happens all too often. However, it is my conviction that Paul's admonition to "be on guard" includes *any departure* from the biblical norms. This was not a theoretical matter for Paul: He forewarned each man—each leader—with anguish and urgency. Specifically, what are we to do?

Peer Reviews

Through timely established reviews, the elder council must reevaluate the biblical qualifications of each of its members, including an assessment of his personal discipline, his family life, reputation in the community, and ministry in the body. This procedure is essential if the standards of elder governance are to be upheld. Paul declares that the *first* requirement for an elder is that he "be above reproach" (1 Tim. 3:2). By keeping its own house in order, the elder council maintains the integrity of its leadership. No doubt there is no more difficult task for elders than requiring one of their own to step down. However, nothing can be more damaging to the leadership of the ruling body than retaining on the council a man who is known to be biblically unfit by all or part of the congregation.

Peer accountability must be exercised in detail, not just in principle.

Peer accountability must be exercised in detail, not just in principle. A formal review process will verify both the elder's maintenance of the biblical character standards, and his diligence in leadership and shepherding. I recommend that this be undertaken at least annually, and not less frequently than review of the church employees' performance. A written report of the review, detailing how the individual satisfies each of the biblical criteria for an elder, and his specific diligence and performance in ministry leadership, should be made available to the Elder Council. After the documentation is reviewed, the council should secure its consensus that each elder is continuing to meet the biblical standards of eldership.

Accountability becomes more difficult for large councils because of the time involved in making a serious attempt to evaluate each elder's life and ministry. Some churches solve this by dividing the council, including staff-elders, into smaller accountability groups which conduct the annual reviews. Redistributing the component members in the groups at intervals will give the elders more exposure to each other and avoid complacency due to familiarity.

Abuse of Power

The last aspect of elder accountability to be touched on here is the procedure to be used whenever a charge of failure is leveled at an elder. If an accusation is brought against a man by two or more witnesses, the council is required by Scripture to investigate the charge fully and impartially, and either to exonerate that elder or to rebuke him for his sin (1 Tim. 5:19–21).

Using the authority of one's position for personal advantage, excluding congregants from (or including them in) activities for political reasons, using a leadership platform to publicly attack an individual, or, the improper application of discipline to punish a certain point of view: These are all forms of abuse.

One of the most egregious forms of the abuse of power is sexual abuse. Each of us hopes this will never occur in our church. However, surveys of pastors reporting on their own behavior indicate that twenty to thirty-five percent have had inappropriate sexual contact with women in their congregations.[36] Since this is a self-confessed statistic, the real percentage is probably much higher.

"Position combined with presence, verbal skill, knowledge, and emotional sway is a phenomenal combination." *Dr. Diane Langberg*

Dr. Diane Langberg, licensed psychologist (with Diane Langberg, Ph.D., and Associates), and adjunct professor of counseling at Westminster Theological Seminary, has had significant experience in treating the victims of such abuse and those in Christian leadership guilty of preying on the very people they are supposed to be shepherding. She observes:

> Position combined with presence, verbal skill, knowledge, and emotional sway is a phenomenal combination. Think about it. You take physical presence, an articulate voice, emotional sway, and theological knowledge, and roll that all together, and then put it in a room with a female (often less powerful than a male), a parishioner (less power in position) whose struggle or pain has rendered them somewhat inarticulate and who is theologically uncertain about some things, and you have a set-up for the abuse of power.[37]

Dr. Langberg has just described the characteristics and skills of an elder, especially one gifted in preaching! Because of the power imbalance in such situations, it is important that the church establish a credible method of safe access to an impartial hearing for anyone who has experienced wrongful treatment by a person in a position of authority in the church. And the congregation must be made aware of this policy. Because of the tragic prevalence of the sexual abuse of women by men in authority, a vital element is that the hearing panel include some members of the same gender as the complainant.

Staff and elders should not be allowed to shield themselves from the council's review by claiming that their accuser has violated the prescribed procedure in Matthew 18. This assertion is invalid for two reasons. First, the offense dealt with in Matthew 18:15–18 is clearly between two individuals and is not a public act or a failure in one's *official* duties. The intent of Matthew 18 is to give the offender the opportunity to repent and to receive forgiveness (when he has wronged an individual) without exposing his fault to undue or ongoing public scrutiny. That privilege—of being protected from exposure—is not available to the elder, vocational or tentmaking, whose personal integrity must match his office. In this case, the violator has sinned against God, his fellow elders, and the congregation, as well as the victim, and does not warrant such protection. Second, since both types of elders are in positions of authority, a power imbalance exists between such a man and a member of the body. The church and its elders themselves will be guilty of abuse if they encourage the victim to incur further risk through *private* confrontation. A policy requiring such an uninformed application of Matthew 18 will ensure that most cases will never be reported. In my firsthand encounters with abusers, Matthew 18 has been offered consistently to prevent exposure and accountability.

Prevention of Abuse

Finally, the key to the prevention of abuse of power is a proactive approach. Each church should have in place policies that address the extreme hazards of the abuse of power in opposite-gender relationships, or in cases of power imbalance between the parties. These occur in counseling, discipling, and supervision. Private meetings should be prohibited between any church leader and a person of the opposite sex outside his immediate family. "Private" means any encounter that is out of view of other responsible church members, such as being alone together in a closed office, or an out-of-the-way restaurant, or when traveling. Also, unmarried leaders must be prohibited from dating anyone they have counseled, supervised, or have been the care giver for in the last twelve months.

Furthermore, no leader who has a strained relationship with his wife, especially if he is unappreciated by her for his ministry efforts and criticized for the amount of time spent in them, should be allowed to counsel or supervise a female. The temptations entailed when a man believes he is being undervalued by his wife, while being admired by a woman from the church, are too unacceptable for the elder and dangerous for the church to risk. Guidelines for these relationships will protect the congregant from an immoral leader, and deter a naive leader from becoming emotionally entangled in an improper relationship. There is no way to mitigate or excuse the grave sinfulness of such conduct, but we do have the means to deter leaders from stepping onto the slippery slope that leads to immoral relationships.

Discipline and Restoration of the Abuser

Can a leader who has been guilty of abuse continue in ministry? If he is removed from his position, can he be restored, and, if so, how soon? The problem is this. A fallen leader no longer meets the elder requirement of being "above reproach." Remorse, repentance, and restitution for his sin, as well as public rebuke, though each is essential, do not restore such a man to being "above reproach" in the eyes of the congregation and the watching world. What is required is the establishment of a new and consistent track record. Scripture specifically warns about haste in these matters. Immediately after commanding that elders who continue in sin be rebuked, Paul says: "Do not lay hands upon anyone [including recommissioning] too hastily and thereby share responsibility for the sins of others" (1 Tim. 5:22).[*]

EXERCISING AUTHORITY

The elder's principal role is that of shepherd-teacher or shepherd-leader. However, he also exercises moral authority in the church. Members should and will turn to elders for direction, for spiritual wisdom and doctrinal insight. At times, elders will be involved in the admonishment of a congregant in his walk, or in counseling in interpersonal difficulties. However, in such circumstances, an individual elder does not speak for the entire council. If his direction is questioned, he should immediately refer the matter to the committee of the council assigned to handle matters of discipline. Members of the congregation should be allowed (with limitations; see Appeals, p. 92) to appeal the decisions of such a committee to the full council.

The congregation must be committed to church discipline in order for that discipline to be effective. The relationship with the church of each attender is best formalized by a member covenant,

---

[*] For a thorough treatment of this subject, see: John H. Armstrong, *Can Fallen Pastors Be Restored? The Church's Response to Sexual Misconduct* (Chicago: Moody, 1995); and Tim LaHaye, *If Ministers Fall, Can They Be Restored?* (Grand Rapids: Zondervan, 1990).

signed when each person joins the church. Such a covenant should include commitment to the principle of submission to the authority of the elders and their discipline. By signing the covenant, the member acknowledges he has understood and agreed to the provisions of the church's bylaws dealing with biblical counseling, confidentiality, conflict resolution, and discipline. This acknowledgment in writing constitutes informed consent and provides reasonable protection of the church from lawsuits arising out of the church's disciplinary efforts. In this regard, it is advisable that the church bylaws and member covenant are reviewed by legal counsel experienced in this area.[*]

By signing the membership covenant, the member acknowledges he has understood and agreed to the provisions of the church's bylaws.

However, many churches have neither a formal membership or have the members sign a membership covenant. It is acknowledged that a covenant is not going to bring about Christian behavior. Its only purpose is to ensure that members understand the church's policies. If one is not used, then special efforts must be made to inform attendees of the policies. Moreover, many people regularly attend our churches but do not become members. When there is overt sin or a conflict is brought before the elders, the church cannot avoid dealing with it simply because those involved are not members. Because of this, provisions of the church bylaws that concern discipline should pertain to both members and nonmembers, and should be routinely communicated to the total congregation, to establish some level of informed consent for the nonmember attendees, and to reduce the church's legal exposure.

Only the decisions of the total body of elders in the local church (the council of elders), reached by consensus, speak for the council. Neither the council moderator, nor any individual elder or staff elder, has any independent official authority, as all are placed on the same level by the fact they are equally under-shepherds of the Chief Shepherd, Jesus Christ. In the words of Peter: "I exhort the elders among you, as your fellow elder. . . . All of you, clothe yourselves with humility toward one another, for God is opposed to the proud,

---

[*] An excellent resource is the consulting service of Peacemaker Ministries, 1537 Avenue D Suite 352, Billings, MT, 59102; 406.256.1583.

but gives grace to the humble" (1 Peter 5:1, 5). The moderator is charged with the responsibilities of maintaining good order and facilitating consensus. He has not been appointed to direct church affairs on his own authority. Between council meetings, he may only communicate the will of the council, not make independent or additional decisions. Similarly, a staff employee has administrative authority only as far as is consistent with the *previous* rulings of the elders, and only within his prescribed job description (Acts 15:1–22).

An elder or staff member who advocates disobedience of the council in the congregation is in rebellion against the Lord's ordained government.

Elders and staff are bound by the decisions of the council. If an elder or staff person is not in agreement with a council determination, he (or she) must make clear his opposition to the council in a spirit consistent with 1 Thessalonians 5:12–13 and Hebrews 13:17. An elder or staff member who advocates disobedience of the council in the congregation is in rebellion against the Lord's ordained government. Therefore, for the well-being of the flock, any such person must be immediately removed from any position of leadership or authority. "For rebellion is as the sin of divination, and insubordination is as iniquity and idolatry" (1 Sam. 15:23). "For there is no authority except from God, and those which exist are established by God. Therefore, whoever resists authority has opposed the ordinance of God; and they who have opposed will receive condemnation upon themselves" (Rom. 13:1–2; cf. Heb. 13:17). The council must be prepared to meet its obligation to protect the flock against such rebellions by having established bylaws and voting procedures that permit the godly majority on the council to act.

As elders we should be continually impressed with the breath and depth of our responsibilities. As this section draws to a close, let us return to our base, our supreme responsibility—maintaining the biblical character standards God holds before each of us, and that must characterize our collective work.

PREREQUISITES FOR GOVERNING BIBLICALLY

The habits of effectively sharing leadership do not come naturally. Governing involves both teamwork and consensus decision-making. At a typical elder council meeting, paid staff elders, who have been working all week juggling many demands in the environment of the church, join forces with tentmaking elders, who have been out in the secular workplace, many in hurried, competitive, and largely non-Christian environments. We cannot expect any of these men suddenly to switch their frames of reference without addressing the core issue of *who they are* and *who they need to be*. On the one hand, as each elder prepares himself for each council meeting, he must check his attitudes and mindset. And, as he convenes each gathering, the moderator must remind his fellow elders of their high calling and serious responsibilities, and of the commensurate perspective and behaviors required.

Moreover, for shared leadership to succeed and for a council to reach godly decisions, each participant must routinely renew his pledge to biblical character standards. The elders' commitment to these should be brought regularly to their attention through a devotion from Scripture, prayer, discussion of a specific norm, or some combination of these methods, to refer to our office, work, and vow. We have promised the Lord, the congregation, and each other to be faithful in:

- Continuing to exhibit the character qualities, stipulated in 1 Timothy 3:1–7 and Titus 1:5–9, that are still required of each man as he continues to serve as an elder. One quality taught in these passages—more than any other—will determine a man's ability to support shared leadership: humility. The proud, "self-willed" individual will never be able to submit his will to that of the council. This task requires extraordinary self-government, which boils down to mastery of one's thoughts and actions.

- Maintaining the primacy of the teaching of the Word, never allowing administrative tasks to crowd out vital personal ministries among God's family. "We will devote ourselves to prayer and to the ministry of the word" (Acts 6:4). "Pay close attention to yourself and your teaching" (1 Tim 4:16).

- Elevating the well-being of Christ's church above one's personal agenda. "Shepherd the church of God which He purchased with His own blood" (Acts 20:28). "Shepherd the flock of God among you . . . according to the will of God" (1 Peter 5:2). "Keep watch over . . . [their] souls as those who will give an account" (Heb. 13:17).

- Maintaining the principle, and demonstrating in behavior, the equality of all elders. "Whoever wishes to become great among you shall be your servant; and whoever wishes to be first among you shall be slave of all" (Mark 10:43–44).

- Loving his brothers and honoring mutual trust. "A new commandment I give to you, that you love one another. . . . By this all men will know that you are My disciples, if you have love for one another" (John 13:34–35). "Beyond all these things put on love, which is the perfect bond of unity" (Col. 3:14).

- Sharing the task. Respecting each elder for his unique gifts; in deference allowing those who are the most gifted, with respect to the issue being addressed, to lead in that case. "According to the measure of Christ's gift, . . . He gave gifts to men" (Eph. 4:7–8).

- Remaining accountable to Christ and to each other. "We proclaim Him, admonishing every man . . . so that we may present every man complete in Christ" (Col. 1:28). "You . . . are . . . able also to admonish one another" (Rom. 15:14). "Be on guard for yourselves" (Acts 20:28). "Bear one another's burdens, and thereby fulfill the law of Christ" (Gal. 6:2).

- Setting aside self-interest to achieve collective decisions, each man carefully monitoring his pride, and checking his opinions lest they have become unquestioned assertions. "Regard one another as more important than yourselves; do not merely look out for your own personal interests, but also for the interests of others" (Phil. 2:3–4).

- Expressing a gentle, patient spirit. "The Lord's bond-servant must not be quarrelsome, but be kind to all, able to teach, patient when wronged, with gentleness correcting those who are in opposition" (2 Tim. 2:24–25).

Yes. "It is a fine work [we] desire to do" (1 Tim. 3:1).

Without consultation, plans are frustrated,
but with many counselors they succeed.
Proverbs 15:22

Chapter 4

The Elder Council

ELDERS ARE CHARGED WITH SERVING AS SHEPHERDS in
various ministries and venues of the church. However,
their collective oversight responsibilities are met through
the decisions they make in the elder council. Therefore, in this
chapter we will examine how this body can achieve its God-given
potential. The elder council will be considered from the
standpoint of its responsibilities, including planning, its size, its
relationship with the staff, and its relationship with the
congregation.

RESPONSIBILITIES OF THE COUNCIL

Many valuable studies have focused on the biblical responsibilities of
each individual elder as he "diligently labor[s] among" God's people
(1 Thess. 5:12). As these responsibilities are so carefully delineated in
the works by Gene Getz, Alexander Strauch, Paul Winslow and
Dorman Followwill, and others,[38] reviewing them here is not
necessary. Instead, the focus will be on the collective responsibilities
of the council.

All agree that elders have a shepherding responsibility.
Nevertheless, elder shepherding is often misconstrued, especially by
clergy, as ancillary leadership, as pertaining exclusively to the care of
individuals or small groups. However, while it is true that shepherds
should be responsive to the needs of individual sheep, their overriding
charge is to lead the flock. Just as in actual pastoral tending of sheep,
the shepherd's duty to the whole flock is not fully expressed in his

care of individual animals. The elders' duty is to lead the church, the entire body.[*]

How then should this divinely appointed collective leadership be expressed? Those that disagree with what we have already set forth (regarding the calling and the appointment of the elders, and the nature of the church) will be led to a false conclusion. Therefore, it is imperative that we reassert that the elder is appointed by the Holy Spirit to shepherd Christ's body, the church. The church is not owned by the congregation. It is Christ's alone: He is the Head (Col. 1:18), and the elders are His stewards. The elders are not elected representatives of the congregation, but are *appointed* representatives of Christ. The elders are responsible *for* the congregation, Christ's flock, not responsible *to* it.

The issue of who owns the church is crucial when we are comparing the functions of the elder council to those of secular institutions from which the church has unadvisedly borrowed forms and terminology. The most common perversion of the elder council's divinely established responsibility occurs when it is operated as a board of directors. This will become apparent when we compare the character of, and rationale for, a corporate board to those of a biblical elder council.

John Carver and Miriam Mayhew Carver, in their definitive work on the functioning of corporate boards,[39] advise such a board to focus on setting policy, and to let the CEO and staff make all the management decisions, within the policies established by the board. Many a senior pastor has seized upon this management method, especially since his position as CEO appears to be enhanced thereby. But, for the church, this approach is both biblically unacceptable and tragic. Both non-profit and for-profit organizations that have owners who are distinct from the management personnel of the organization must have boards of directors. The reason is that an organization's paid staff cannot be trusted *on its own* to represent the interests of the owners (the owners being the stockholders in the case of a for-profit organization, or donors in the case of a non-profit organization). The managers must be supervised by an independent board. (For instance,

---

[*] Since a church is a nonprofit corporation and may own property, the council may also serve as the legally recognized, responsible body of the corporation. Usually the council's officers are designated as the officers of the corporation; however, once the church is established, the satisfaction of the legal requirements is a small task and should not distort the shepherding character of the council, or distract it from concentrating on the spiritual health of the flock.

the management is not allowed to set its own performance standards or salaries; a board is needed to establish these on behalf of the owners.) This is in marked contrast to those entities whose owners *are* the managers; in that case, a board of directors is not needed (for instance, in a family business whose owners are the managers, or in a law firm directed by its senior partners). A biblical church falls in the later category, because, as God's stewards, the elders collectively function as the owner.

In a church with biblical eldership, the elder council cannot be a corporate board of directors. There are fundamental differences between the two:

BIBLICAL ELDER COUNCIL	BOARD OF DIRECTORS
The council is accountable to, and represents God, the Owner, and is not responsible to the congregation.	The board serves, and is responsible to, the owners (the stockholders or donors).
The elders manage as active leaders and shepherds.	The individual directors are passive managers.
Each elder on the council is an actual ministry participant. He manages from a base of direct experience in the body.	The individual directors are outsiders with no involvement in the entity's actual operations.
The council is assisted in its tasks by staff when necessary.	The board of directors carries out all operations through its essential staff.
The church does not have a CEO because all its elders are equal in authority.	The board of directors elects a CEO who is then accountable only to that board.
Staff elders, along with tent-making elders, hold one another mutually accountable for their active leadership for the health of the church.	Corporate staffs are rewarded (or not) through salary increases and bonuses, based on meeting standards set by the outside passive directors.

In sum, the Carvers' advice is appropriate for those organizations whose owners are separate from the leadership. However, it is a gravely misguided blueprint for a church led by biblical elders. We must not surrender the elders' biblical mandate of active ministry leadership by allowing our elder councils to become bodies that function as boards of directors, composed of passive managers.

Having established the elder council's collective, overall responsibility to lead the church, let us delve into how the elders can do this effectively. What decisions should be made collectively by the council and what decisions can be left to individual elders or staff members? I maintain that, to be biblical, all decisions that affect the church must be made collectively by the elders. Christ's will for the church is only found in this manner. However, this does not mean that every decision requires a meeting of the council. The council can delegate to individual elders and individual staff members (or to committees or commissions) authority to make decisions within predetermined, acceptable limits and in accordance with previously established elder policies. However, no individual should be placed in the position, or place himself in the position, of making decisions for the church. For example, an elder can tell a couple whether the church will marry them, based upon the couple's meeting (or not meeting) the criteria the council has previously established. However, that elder, by himself, may not grant an exception to the church's policy on marriage.

While it is appropriate in churches that have employees for the staff to coordinate their own activities, elder governance is subverted when the staff meets apart from the council to make decisions affecting the church. In a biblical church, the staff is charged with performing specified professional tasks for the council. It may not supplant the council as a leadership body. I will discuss the ability of the council to provide the required leadership under The Size Dilemma, page 83.

The elder council must be proactive, not simply reactive, to challenges as they occur.

The issue of who makes decisions is greatly alleviated if the council is forward-looking in its deliberations rather than being primarily reactive to emerging situations. By taking responsibility for the church's future, the council can lay down clear guidance for those delegated to carry out the council's leadership-decisions for the church. Obviously, elders must conduct oversight of current church affairs and make time-critical decisions. However, the efforts of the council will be much more productive if the men have invested the time in prayerfully charting the future of the church. The elder council must be proactive, not simply reactive, to challenges as they occur.

At the outset, leadership must take into account the perspectives provided by three time periods: the church's past, its present, and its future. Oversight requires that the council review what the church has accomplished for the Lord in the past, its failures, and the lessons learned from that history. This is consistent with the careful practice established in Old Testament times of setting forth a detailed history of Israel's past and the analysis of that history by the prophets. Israel was supposed to remember always both the lessons learned from God's intervention, and from their own successes and failures in following His leading.

Planning for the church's future is so critical to the health of the church that the next chapter will be devoted to that aspect of the council's work. However, first we must address several issues that affect the council's ability to carry out its task: its size, and its relationships to staff and to the congregation.

SIZE OF THE ELDER COUNCIL

The elder council must see that all the needs of the congregation are addressed, either directly by the council members, or through the people and structures it puts in place and continues to oversee. The council's primary collective tasks are oversight of the current life of the body and leading the congregation into its future. How large should the elder council be in order to meet these obligations?

SMALL CHURCHES

In smaller churches, the availability of a limited number of qualified men may be the controlling factor determining elder council size. (Note that the apostles were not a governing body; consequently, no biblical precedence for the choice of the number twelve exists.) On the other hand, the elder council must not be so small that it is controlled by one person, or that it becomes an elite group that violates the principle that governing is to be by a plurality of elders who are equal in authority and sufficiently diverse to assure independent thinking.

An example of an elite group is the elder council composed of a small number of men picked by their pastor because of their loyalty to him, rather than for their elder qualities and ministry leadership. Another instance is the elder council consisting only of paid staff.

Since the elders are charged with the oversight of the entire church, a variety of firsthand knowledge in their ranks is essential. In my experience, it has been illuminating to observe the creative tensions between those elders who are engineers and others who are salesmen. The salesmen believe anything is possible and are eager to proceed. Not so certain, the engineers first require a full understanding of the whats, hows, and whys, before embarking. The end result can be a careful but aggressive plan for accomplishing the task, and a display of God's purpose in providing a diversity of gifts.

While two constitutes plurality, practically speaking, at least four men are required. A council must be large enough to assure that decisions are the result of the thoughtful discussion of men who have prayerfully and independently considered the wisdom of a course of action. Therefore, the man who leads a small church, or desires to plant a church with biblical governance, must avoid solo leadership. Rather, at the outset, he must establish peer relationships with other men who will share the ministry and elder leadership of the church. Turning the troops around is very hard once they have been led down the wrong course.

LARGE CHURCHES

In larger churches, the opposite problem may crop up, that is, not too few qualified elders, but too many for the council to be effective. Biblical governance by a plurality of elders is assured through the active involvement of elders, not by their sheer number. The pastor of a very large church (in the thousands) once told me that he had seventy-five elders who met four times a year. Puzzled, I asked what he called this form of governance. With a big grin, he answered, "Benevolent dictatorship."

The quantity of elders should be established by the number of qualified men the Lord calls.

Those who base their case on the nature of group dynamics insist that, for the sake of productive meetings, there is an upper limit on the number who may serve on a leadership team. I agree that effective groups have an upper size limit, depending on the function of each group. (I will suggest later, under The Size Dilemma, page 83, how to conform the leadership team to a viable size.) However, two factors that we have already established militate against restricting the total number of elders to an arbitrary number. First, the size of the church should not determine how many elders are on the council. Instead, the quantity should be established by the number of qualified men the Lord calls to be elders. Scripture states that men should aspire to eldership (1 Tim. 3:1), and that they are appointed by the Holy Spirit

(Acts 20:28). Therefore, those who aspire to eldership, are performing the functions of elders, and are biblically qualified should be formally recognized, thereby providing that congregation with its total component of elders.

Notice the biblical pattern we are given. The apostles *first* ascertained those who were already doing the work and leading required of elders, and who were otherwise qualified. *Then* they appointed these men elders. There is no hint of a selection process, resulting in a predetermined number being chosen out of all who were ministering *and* were fully qualified. Today, in like manner, those who are qualified and are teaching, shepherding, and leading in the congregation should be recognized as being elders. This method proceeds from Paul's instructions: "We request of you, brethren, that you appreciate *those who diligently labor among you*, and *have charge over you* in the Lord and *give you instruction* [admonish you], and that you esteem them very highly in love *because of their work*" (1 Thess. 5:12–13, italics added).

The second argument against limiting the number of elders in a large church is the vital need all ministries have for elder leadership. Elders exercise oversight through, and because of, their active participation in ministries (and not simply as members of an isolated board performing some form of supposedly representative government). As a church grows, its programs expand and multiply. They all call for active leadership. A church could continue to add paid staff, but this increases its burgeoning and lopsided budget, and exacerbates the church's failure to develop internal leadership. Or, the church can inspire tentmaking elders to supply the leadership! The ratio of staff expense per attendee, on an inflation-corrected basis, cannot be allowed to increase (except in the first years of its development) if the church is to grow. The alternative is preferable. This ratio should decrease as the incumbent leadership becomes more proficient in training volunteers to lead.

PREPARING FOR GROWTH

Since the biblical pattern—and still our present mandate—is to replicate leadership, we need to be continually preparing men for eldership. If a church intends to grow, obviously it must train more leadership. If a church intends to plant churches, enough elders to equip the new bodies with effective seasoned leadership must be trained.

My work with church plants has led me to conclude that the limitation on growth through church planting is not financial but the availability of tested leaders. Some of the people most willing to leave an established church to support a church plant may do so out of mixed or unrealistic motives. The stability of the church plant is primarily dependent on the wisdom and dependability of its initial leadership. Therefore, the new body needs seasoned elders. Many newly formed churches experience failure and messy splits because they were started with bursts of energy and enthusiasm, but were not founded on the godly maturity of a core of experienced men.

THE SIZE DILEMMA

As the church grows and the number of elders increases beyond a few, a dramatic and troubling alteration impinges on the quality of debate and interaction in council meetings. From our own experiences in the past, we have seen that an informal meeting of five to seven men can prove highly productive because of the uninhibited exchange—much more profitable than the formal meeting of a larger number. Although it is theoretically possible for an elder council larger than seven members to deliberate thoughtfully, the obstacles to doing so become increasingly difficult to surmount. What's more, skillful facilitation of the deliberative process is then absolutely crucial. Though not a biblical consideration, this number seven is simply a practical limit, based on years of personal experience, the considerations given below, and many studies of the dynamics of deliberative groups.[40]

The large council cannot produce creative answers to problems—and it cannot lead.

Several aspects of the size dilemma need to be highlighted here. First, too many men on the council limits debate. Productive debate requires the back-and-forth clarification of an issue by all speakers involved. The length of deliberation needed to achieve a consensus decision is directly proportional to the number of men involved. Simply asking each elder for his opinion before voting is not deliberation. For example, say fifteen men were to speak, each only once for five minutes, one round could take a full hour and fifteen minutes. Such a procedure is not satisfactory for producing the consensus of all. An alternative, negative outcome is that most of the council elders will remain passive while only a few participate in the debate. Therefore, when councils exceed the seven member limit, and they must in larger churches, the council can no longer act (and should not act) as a committee of the whole, trying to work out solutions to the church's issues.

THE ELDER COUNCIL

The second and third features of a large council are integrally connected. The large council cannot produce creative answers to problems and it cannot lead. While a large governing body can easily ratify a matter presented to it for a decision, any council numbering over seven is ill-suited to *create* solutions. A huge difference can be seen in the quality of a plan created by a small skillful team (and later ratified by the larger body) and that created by a large group acting as a committee-of-the-whole.

In Scripture, elders are described as ruling (leading) the church. Because exchange of opinions, thoughtful discussion, and focused prayer are all required in leading, there is a practical limitation on the number of elders involved in the decision-making of the church's council. Michael Doyle and David Straus agree that, regardless of venue, when a group exceeds seven, informal discussion of complex issues is impossible.[41] Certainly, a council of more than seven cannot meet often enough, or discuss issues sufficiently to lead its church. As a body, they cannot stay on top of the decision stream required to manage the day-to-day needs of the church or creatively address the future.

George Barna sets even lower limits for an effective group than I advise:

> A large group cannot lead. Anyone who has been involved in effective leadership knows that once a team gets beyond six people, it becomes unwieldy and degenerates into compromises that reflect the lowest common denominator. At that stage, the focus of the group is not upon a commonly held vision but upon producing some tangible outcome with which everyone is comfortable. That is not leadership, it is accommodation. Effective leadership teams typically have three to five people. Less than three leaves you without the horsepower to get the job done. More than five produces inefficiencies and excessive compromise.[42]

Consequently and sadly, as its size grows beyond seven, an elder council degenerates into a passive board of directors, usually mere observers of the work of a professional staff. The council itself recognizes that, because of its unwieldy size, it cannot effectively manage the church, and most of the men would be unwilling to spend the time required to do so anyway. Therefore, in many large churches councils take a step that is completely unsanctioned in Scripture: they hire professionals to do their job. They sidestep their biblical mandate to govern.

DELEGATION

Providentially, there is an alternative that preserves and supports the biblical role of the elders and of the council—*delegation*. Since a large council cannot lead or manage the dynamic life of the church, it must delegate the day-to-day direction of the church and the coordination of its ministries to a leadership team, and the direction of specific ministries to commissions.

AUTHORIZING A SMALLER LEADERSHIP TEAM

Even when the individual ministries of the church have been delegated to smaller teams, the role of a large council in leading the overall church is still a matter of concern. If the Lord provides a large number of qualified elders, the council size dilemma can be resolved by some form of delegation, from the total governing body of elders to a smaller leadership team, consisting of five to seven elders. Stephen Robbins sums up the conclusions of many studies of organizational behavior.

> Large groups—with a dozen or more members—are good for gaining diverse input. So, if the goal of the group is fact-finding, larger groups should be more effective. On the other hand, smaller groups are better at doing something productive with that input. Groups of approximately seven members, therefore, tend to be more effective for taking action.[43]

One caution. Those elders who are not on the leadership team still retain their biblical governing authority. There is no such thing as an elder who does not share in governing responsibility. However, there must be a division of labor. The major body of elders in the church— the council—must be fully informed of the work of the leadership team and approve any of its decisions that have a major effect on the direction of the church's ministry. At the same time, the council must hold the leadership team accountable for execution of the direction *the council* has previously approved, and for the coordination of the ministries *it* has chartered. Also, as previously mentioned, our standard of biblical governance dictates that the size of the delegated body should not be so few as to constitute an oligarchy, or ruling elite, or be dominated by staff members.

If such a solution—the delegation to a smaller body—is chosen, four commonsense policies are pivotal. First, those elders of the council who are not serving on the leadership team must stand by the delegation they have made by trusting and respecting its work. They have chosen these brother elders for the leadership team because they are the men most gifted in leadership and administration. Council elders must be willing to let the delegated body lead under the council's overall oversight.

The leadership team is *not* a separate legislative body.

Second, communication is vital. Council elders have to be kept informed of the work of the leadership team; they must receive adequate minutes of meetings, and be apprized of agendas of upcoming meetings and the issues being studied or discussed. Also, all elders should be free to attend any sessions of the leadership team, as long as they refrain from interactions that would impede its deliberations, and abide by the set agenda of the meeting. If any elder has concerns, he should handle them in a way that will maximize the effectiveness of the leadership team. If all the elders are careful to continue to contribute their regular attendance at called meetings of the council, the arrangement will remain healthy. Part of elders' responsibilities includes this two-way street: participation in ministry that informs the total work of the elders in the church, and participation in council meetings that shapes the work of their ministries.

The third rule to be followed is crucial. The elders should not create a structure that could be construed as the church's having *two* legislative bodies, or a bicameral government, such as the Senate and the House of Representatives of the United States Congress. Instead, the total council of elders *contains* the smaller leadership team. The leadership team is *not* a separate legislative body.

Success will largely depend on compliance with the fourth rule. On the leadership team, tentmaking elders must be permanent players, just as are the staff elders. Moreover, tentmaking elders serving on the leadership team must be chosen with the same care as staff elders who are responsible for preaching, and they must be equally committed to the task of leading the church. The service of bivocational members on the leadership team must not be viewed as temporary assignment. The same consideration applies here as was previously discussed under elder term limits. If paid staff have permanent positions but tentmaking elders are rotated, the employees will determine the direction and work of the church, thereby subverting true elder governance.

THE ELDER COUNCIL

It is the normal and necessary practice in a staff-run church for its leadership to meet at least once a week. An equal commitment is required of the tentmaking elders on a leadership team in an elder-led church. And this is in addition to each elder's fulfilling his ministry leadership responsibilities. Many will say that this is asking too much of a man who is not a vocational elder (on staff or paid). Indeed, this will be too much for a man who misunderstands biblical eldership and desires a position on a council that resembles a secular board of directors. However, the true elder— the man who has been called by the Holy Spirit to ministry leadership—will be willing to commit to such an effort and to shoulder such responsibility.

On the issue of names for the elders' bodies, since the overall responsibility for the church rests upon all the elders, the larger body should retain the name of Council. Then a serviceable term, such as Action Team or Leadership Team, may be employed for the smaller delegated group. I do not consider it wise to use business terminology like "board" or "executive" as these words lead to distortions of the perception of the elders' true service.

**If the council fails to delegate,
the oversight of the church is effectively halted.**

The responsibility for the oversight of the entire church remains with the full council. In its entirety, it can and must continue to pray for the congregation, hear ministry reports, and ratify the carefully worked out solutions crafted by the leadership team, assigned committees, or ministry commissions. But some decisions are so important to the church that they will require the deliberation of the entire council. (Each council will need to decide the degree of delegation it will make to its leadership team and what issues must be brought back to the full council for a decision.) These determinations are more easily made if each matter is considered ahead of time by a designated or ad hoc committee. This task group, coordinating with the leadership team and working on its own prior to the meeting of the council, carefully explores the issue, praying for wisdom, interviewing those involved, and sorting out the facts. Once the committee has agreed to and prepared a proposal or report, the matter is referred to the full council. This delegation of the *creative* functions of the council— problem-solving and planning—is a critical concept. It has many applications and ramifications, some of which are delineated below.

If the council fails to delegate, the oversight of the church is effectively halted. For instance, if the council is consumed with dealing with an ongoing issue, such as a discipline problem (that could best be handled by a few elders), the priority work of the council is thwarted. Therefore, if it is important or time-critical that the whole council (of more than seven members) design the resolution of an issue, formal facilitation of the discussion is required. However, such discussions should be avoided, except in emergency situations and on issues that require the entire council's participation. This matter is taken up later, under Handling the Major Decisions (p. 142).

Many argue that groups, no matter how small, cannot lead. They are half right. A group can very effectively choose a course of action, but the articulation of this course of action can only be effectuated through individual leaders. A group cannot persuade others to follow. Persuasion must be undertaken by individual leaders, each leading the staff and congregation in his area of gifting and concentration. In this way, the council will not be speaking to the congregation through a single spokesman, or sounding like a choir singing in unison. Rather, the council will have several spokesmen—each speaking for the council in his area of congregational leadership—somewhat like the contributions of a variety of soloists. The biblical model is not a single leader but a plurality of leaders who have found God's direction for His people.

Just as the church needs effective, overall leadership, so too is the council responsible for giving its individual ministries effective direction. Once the church grows to the extent that the elder council cannot provide hands-on leadership for each and all ministries, delegation to ministry commissions is appropriate. I prefer the term "commission," because it conveys the sense of specific appointment and delegation.

COMMISSIONS AND MINISTRY TEAMS

Delegation should be looked upon as the necessary response to the Lord's provision of diverse gifts in the council. Paul speaks of the special gifts given to the church in Romans 12:4–8, Ephesians 4:11, and 1 Corinthians 12:14–30. In each case, the diversity of gifts is for the benefit of the church. Our response should be to honor diversification as truly beneficial.

This benefit must be emphasized, especially as it runs counter to our sinful, usual practice and mindset. Consequently, we fail to understand or include men unlike ourselves. When this occurs, we need to call this narrow-mindedness by its rightful name—dishonor. God's gifts to the church are "for the equipping of the saints for the work of service, to the building up of the body of Christ, . . . from whom the whole body, being fitted and held together by what every joint supplies, according to the proper working of each individual part, causes the growth of the body for the building up of itself in love (Eph. 4:12–16). Each part "supplies" something necessary and we ought to see to its "proper working." Or, in imitation of our Lord, we are to "walk in love" (Eph. 5:1–2).

Clearly, the obligation that flows from God's provision of manifold gifts is that management of specific ministry areas must be delegated. Once elders are assigned such accountability, the entire council must then allow itself to be kept informed by those elders most involved or most gifted in those particular ministry areas. In a moderate-sized church, the elders will know and understand the totality of the church's work. But, in large churches, the elder council may have many members, men who are each specializing in a few ministries. As a result, many elders will not be well-acquainted with areas of service other than their own, and may not be equipped to understand the intricacies of one another's concerns. Therefore, especially when decisions must be made in those areas, the council should defer to those men it has put in charge. It would be unwise and inappropriate for a majority of council elders to assert arbitrary control over any area in which they are not involved.

The example of the Apostle Paul guides us: he instructed the elders in doing things he himself knew intimately and practiced repeatedly. In Acts 20 he establishes his credentials for instructing the elders in their ministry responsibilities by stating his own extensive, personal involvement in this kind of elder service, "teaching you publicly and from house to house" (v. 20).

In a small church the council may be able to directly supervise and direct all the ministries. However as a church grows the quality of oversight deteriorates if the council attempts to provide the needed leadership across a large number of ministries. In such a case, delegation is prudent. Many small churches fail to reach their communities for Christ or to meet their own spiritual needs precisely because of their elders' unwillingness to delegate.

Apart from a leadership team, delegation is usually managed by establishing permanent commissions which oversee the church's ministries. These groups can work more efficiently than the whole council for two reasons: their smaller size and composition. Each commission should be composed of those personally involved in that ministry or area and equipped with the requisite background. If a commission is constituted largely of nonparticipants in that ministry, they will be essentially directing someone else's ministry. They will be passive managers, instead of the actual leader-participants, and the commission will be impotent. Again, George Barna's insights are instructive:

> Teams are most effective when they are created in response to a shared commitment to a specific outcome. Too often churches develop teams on the basis of preexisting friendships, scheduling convenience, or church politics. Teams are useful when there is mutual dependence among the members, because they understand that their cooperation creates synergy: they can accomplish more by working together than by working solo. The teams that gain ground for the kingdom are the ones based on purposeful productivity—that is, the individuals on the team are together because their combination of skills, gifts, and talents unlocks opportunities that would otherwise go unexploited.[44]

In every case, even for a temporary or ad hoc committee, it is wise for the assignment to be formalized in a charter that originates from the ministry team, is coordinated by the leadership team, and is ratified by the council. For a permanent commission, this charter should define the scope of the group's mandate to manage and advance the particular ministry, thus giving its leadership the flexibility to function autonomously within the parameters of its charter. For an ad hoc group, a similar statement will determine its area of investigation, term of service, and the like. Failure to use a charter will lead to misunderstandings over responsibility and authority. Such a guiding charter need be only two pages long, and the effort to establish it is valuable. A charter always "exists"; the questions are—was it written up and does everyone agree on its scope?

Each ministry should be *self-governed* by a management team of its leaders and ministry participants, within the guidelines of its council-approved charter. Just as functioning as a team of equals is essential and biblical for the council, equality of authority and responsibility among the ministry's participants is essential. Much greater involvement in, and ownership of, the ministries of the church by its people are realized by this method than by the more traditional, top-down approach of hierarchical control. In the latter, with its top-down implementation of decisions, such directives are not necessarily sanctioned or adopted (owned) by the rank and file. And it is certainly extremely difficult to move valuable input *up* the system.

Nonparticipants will be needed on the management teams in at least two areas: worship and employee relations. For the worship management team, a critical leadership committee, it is appropriate to include elders who may not be involved in actual preaching, leading, or performing, but who are knowledgeable in these areas of service. The employee relations committee handles the administration relationship between the employer—the church—and its employees. Therefore, such a committee should be composed primarily of elders who are not on staff. However, representation by one or two key staff supervisors or the director of administration is beneficial.

Church discipline matters should be delegated to a permanent commission, or, on a case-by-case basis, to ad hoc committees for the following reasons (among others):

- Because of the time commitment required for each discipline process, very little prompt and effective discipline will be carried out in the church if each situation must be handled by the full council.

- The purposes of discipline are to resolve conflict or to restore individuals. Requiring the accused to testify in front of the full council is not compatible with, or conducive to, either purpose.

- Discipline requires the careful gathering of facts, the interviewing of individuals, and hearings.

- The maintenance of confidentiality cannot be guaranteed to persons appearing in a council meeting, since both members' notes and the minutes of the meeting can be subpoenaed by a court; for instance, for a divorce hearing. On the other hand, it is highly probably that the assertion of privilege for a committee performing a "pastoral function" would be sustained by a court.

Finally, the delegation of the financial administration of the church deserves special attention. Some churches have a separate board of trustees to manage the church's finances, because it is thought expedient to relieve the elders of the distraction of financial affairs. However, no New Testament precedent exists for a board of trustees at the same level as the elder council. Who is to mediate between them when there is a disagreement? Experience has shown that having two such boards can create an adversarial predicament: the elders who have a vision for expanding the Lord's work lock in conflict with the trustees who are trying to conserve resources. Ken

Sande, of Peacemaker Ministries, tells of incidents in which trustees and elders of the same church have sued each other.[45]

When the council sets aside the detailed management of finances, it should be assigned to a subordinate finance committee, thus avoiding the potential of a power struggle. However, the elders should not divorce themselves from the obligation of establishing the church's overall financial policies, including setting the size of the overall budget and its major categories. Moreover, having established budgets, the elders, as part of their teaching mandate, must not defer to others the task of challenging the congregation to maintain biblical stewardship. Oversight responsibility, separated from encouragement of the stewardship that makes ministry possible, is unwise and counterproductive.

APPEALS

Since commissions and committees are subordinate to the council, anyone who is dissatisfied with a decision at the lower level may appeal the decision to the full council. However, the council should set rules to limit such appeals strictly to those that deserve a hearing before the full body. If the council does not follow this practice, the authority of the ancillary delegated groups will be destroyed. Moreover, the council, acting as a committee of the whole, will be consumed with such matters, and valuable time will be shunted away from the council's efforts to cover its priorities.

The following procedure guarantees protection to any individual who feels ill-served by a commission or committee, and, at the same time, filters out those appeals without merit. The council must require a written request for an appeal hearing. Then the appeal should be heard only if the council determines that evidence exists that the appointed body acted improperly or on inadequate information. Otherwise, the council should decline to hear the appeal, thus sustaining the decision of the subordinate committee.

DELEGATION ENHANCES OVERSIGHT

Delegation does not relieve the elder council of its oversight responsibility for the whole church. In reality, proper, well-handled, authorized delegation makes oversight a reality. The elders who are personally involved in a particular specialty—and part of that ministry's management team or supervising committee—will be overseeing thereby that portion of the church's effort for the entire council. This oversight is extended to the entire council as these men report at regular intervals on the health and current direction of their ministries.

Because of enthusiastic ownership of the Lord's work and available volunteers, tentmaking and otherwise, many small churches do not need salaried elders or staff. Sometimes it is because of limited finances. However, in most larger churches, the elders find it prudent to hire some of their number to serve full time as staff. In addition, as the church grows, full-time administrative staff and some ministry specialists are needed. However, in these transitions, great care must be taken to avoid diluting the biblical role of the elders.

RELATING TO AND RECRUITING STAFF

At some point in a church's growth, augmentation of the elder and volunteer leadership with salaried staff is judicious. However, this immediately places the biblical character of the church in peril. Clearly, the working relationship of the elder council with the church's salaried staff is of utmost importance, but when staff is added, the elders' active biblical role must be maintained. Regrettably, in many situations, hired staff is given responsibility for the operations of the church, and the elders are relegated to being only in charge of overall goals. This is what I call the "no middle" approach. This course is often chosen as their final line of defense by those who want a clergy-controlled church.

The "no middle" method confines elders to the top—a board with no operational duties—and to the bottom—elders leading small Bible studies and making member visits—while restricting all ministry leadership to the "professionals." The model of paying salaried staff to lead the church under the supervision of a board is not a biblical model. The elders are supposed to be the ones who "diligently labor among you" (1 Thess. 5:12), and they certainly are those who "keep watch over your souls as those *who will give an account*" (Heb. 13:17, italics added). George Barna adds empirical evidence:

> One of the most impressive—and important—elements of leadership in the highly effective churches is that most of the leadership comes from the laity. Analysts often focus on the abilities of the pastor, but we find that every highly effective church is able to exploit opportunities and overcome obstacles because of the depth of its lay leadership.[46]

THE ELDER COUNCIL

Due to limitations on the availability of tentmakers' time, supplementing the efforts of volunteers with paid staff may be the prudent choice for larger churches; this means putting some elders on salary and hiring ministry assistants of various kinds. However, the fact that some elders are volunteers and others paid should not place them on different and, sometimes, adversarial terms. Instead, the management structure beneath the elder council should involve an integration of volunteers and staff, with no fixed relationship between supervisors and those under them based on who is salaried and who is not. Staff meetings, retreats, off-sites, and workshops that do not involve the bivocational elders are destructive of the relationship that must be maintained between paid staff and tentmakers.

There is a loss of the unique biblical character of the church as its leadership becomes professionalized.

As a church grows, maintaining its distinctive character, biblical eldership, and commitment to team ministry is a great challenge. Many brothers have described (and I have witnessed firsthand) the loss of the unique biblical character of the church as its leadership becomes professionalized. If candidates for paid staff positions can be found within the congregation—those who possess the required skills and are already committed to the biblical view of the church—a much better outcome is possible. Far better to use a known, internal candidate of unquestioned character and loyalty to the church's goals than to bring in a nominee from outside, one with unquestionable skills, but unproven commitment to the church's philosophy of ministry. Especially is this true when employing seminary graduates, since most seminaries are firmly in the grip of those who espouse clerical control of the church. Where theological training is required, church personnel can take seminary courses concurrent with their employment. Consultants can be brought in to enrich and coach employees in their responsibilities. Always, we should fully explore the option of developing our own people before going outside.

When reaching outside the local body is necessary, a careful procedure is warranted to assure that the church's needs are met and that the integrity of its vision is not violated. A comprehensive job description is prerequisite to starting any search. Besides clearly listing the responsibilities of the position, the description must delineate the reporting and teamwork relationships. Also, selection criteria should be prepared to guide the search process. When the search committee has the selection criteria before any interviews take place, the personalities of candidates are less likely to overly influence the selection procedure. Neither the selection guidelines nor the church's philosophy of ministry should be revealed to prospective employees: If they are, the interviewees will color their presentations to fit the criteria. During interviews, it is amazing how many candidates say that they agree 100 percent with a church's philosophy of ministry, but, after being hired, will try to impose new agendas.

The only reliable predictor of the prospect's future performance is the information gained from careful reference checks.

Although much can be learned from the interview, the only reliable predictor of the prospect's future performance is the information gained from careful reference checks obtained from those who have observed his previous ministry. Such reference checks should not be limited to those persons suggested by the candidate, and they must provide a 360-degree view—from his supervisors, peers, and those he led. In evaluating references, emphasis must be fixed on the candidate's character, as it always carries more weight than his skills.

By the time a candidate is found—one who appears to fill the job description and has impressed the search committee—the committee will be suffering from search fatigue and pressure to fill the position, and very hopeful that the prospect will receive favorable reference checks. In effect, the search committee is the group *least equipped* psychologically for conducting the reference checks! Investigations of failed staff have repeatedly revealed that search committees neglected to heed warnings from references, or verify information that the candidates had character flaws, or were committed to ministry philosophies that would clash with that of the church. The explanation is that our natural tendency is to hear the positive, and downplay the adverse.

Frequently, while I was an aerospace manager, I was indicated as a reference by one of my employees being recruited by another company. Shortly into the ensuing telephone call, during his inquiries about my employee's strengths and weaknesses, it became obvious that the man calling had already made up his mind. He intended to make the hire and was just satisfying his company's internal requirement of making a reference check. For these reasons, many of us strongly recommend that reference checks be done by other qualified, but disinterested, persons who have not participated in the search process, perhaps a professional not in the church.

If the new employee will be involved in counseling or finances, and almost all will be, or working with youth or children, a criminal background check is imperative. Failure to obtain one will expose the church to litigation, if in the future a problem occurs.

RELATIONSHIP WITH THE CONGREGATION

The council is biblically obligated to shepherd the flock through effective leadership and teaching. This responsibility is not solely in the hands of the elder or elders gifted in preaching. It belongs to the *whole* council, and is expressed in its members' hands-on involvement in the church body.

**The elders' chief avenue for leading
is the teaching ministry of the church.**

The Lord holds the elders, both collectively and individually, responsible for teaching and guiding the congregation. The body cannot lead itself or initiate proposals: it must be led. To that end, after the elder council has found Christ's will for the church (through congregational input, study, prayer, and discussion), it must—at every opportunity—put that biblically derived direction before the congregation.

The elders' chief avenue for leading is the teaching ministry of the church. Therefore, its elders should be found interacting with— leading—God's family in various teaching venues. As Scripture is expounded and applied, the people should not only be challenged in their individual lives, but they should develop a community sense of the congregation's collective biblical purpose. If led well by its elders, the church as a whole will take ownership of that particular work God is calling them to undertake in their "Jerusalem, . . . and even to the remotest part of the earth" (Acts 1:8).

COMMUNICATION

The logical venue for communicating the church's purpose is that time when the congregation is gathered together for worship and teaching, as the largest percentage of attendees is reached at that time. In this congregational setting, God's people are called to be united behind the overall focus of the church. Emphasizing God's intent for His church cannot be thought to detract from worship, because affirming His will is a part of worship. Worship leaders who object to allocating the time should understand this priority: Believers must express unity of purpose in more ways than joining in praise and song. Alexander Strauch says:

> As teachers and defenders of the Word, the elders need to be about the great business of the church's beliefs and mission. That means that a fundamental task of the elder council is to define, clarify, state, and continually restate the church's foundational, nonnegotiable beliefs, its unique doctrinal distinctives, its ministry priorities, its direction, its spiritual values, and its mission and vision.[47]

Consistent with Strauch's exhortation is the example of the renowned preacher, John Piper, who devoted *eleven* consecutive weeks to preaching on the mission and vision of Bethlehem Baptist Church in Minneapolis.[48]

Despite the crucial importance of the worship service for communication, this format does not provide for interaction. Usually people cannot receive detailed information, ask questions of the leadership, and engage in the dialogue that is so critical to individuals taking ownership. For this reason, other venues, such as congregational meetings, publications, and small assemblies, must supplement what is accomplished in the worship services.

Congregational business meetings should not be limited to voting on church matters but be used to remind and teach the members of the purpose and vision of the church. Although limited question and answer activity can take place, because of the number of people present, this venue does not provide the best opportunity for two-way communication, especially as the church grows. In addition, in larger churches, having more than twenty-five percent of the membership present is unusual. Newsletters and church web pages can attempt to reach the other seventy-five percent, but, again, they do not provide for two-way communication.

**Individual attention trumps any
other communication device.**

Consequently, a distributed communication approach involving all the elders is essential: Elders fluent in explaining the intricacies of the church's biblically-derived purpose and direction, spread over the width of the body, interacting and connecting with the flock. Adult Sunday school classes, informational forums, leadership meetings, and, especially, small groups in homes, provide the configurations in which the elders may effectively lead the congregation. These occasions provide for personalized teaching and exchange in informal and nonconfrontational environments, and make up the deficits of other communication methods. Individual attention trumps any other communication device.

CONGREGATIONAL OBLIGATIONS

As communication must be two-way, God's people must take up their responsibility to participate actively. Scripture instructs believers to respect their leadership: "We request of you, brethren, that you *appreciate* those who diligently labor among you, and have charge over you in the Lord and give you instruction, and that you *esteem* them very highly in love because of their work" (1 Thess. 5:12–13, italics added). Too often, members grumble and gossip about their concerns and unanswered questions when they should be bringing these to individual elders for clarification. The elders need the help of the eyes and ears of the body.* Besides offering respect, members must *obey* the leadership: "Obey your leaders and submit to them, for they keep watch over your souls as those who will give an account. Let them do this with joy and not with grief, for this would be unprofitable for you" (Heb. 13:17). This assumes that the body is led by true elders who do "diligently labor," who are interested in and involved with the sheep.

These two congregational obligations to the elders, appreciation and obedience, support a third, that of protecting the integrity of the leadership. If any member has information confirmed by another witness (or several), suggesting that a church leader is guilty of dishonesty, immorality, or any other violation of his being "above reproach," he or she must report this to the elder council. This can be done carefully and privately by speaking or writing to a council member. In such a case, the elder council is obligated to investigate, and either clear or discipline the accused: "Do not receive an accusation against an elder except on the basis of two or three witnesses. Those who continue in sin, rebuke in the presence of all, so that the rest also will be fearful of sinning" (1 Tim. 5:19–20).

The congregation has several responsibilities derived from the privilege of the Christian community and from being members of the body of Christ. In addition to those mentioned above, they include some form of identification with the local body (some call this formal

---

* To assist in rumor control, to keep track of the hurting sheep who need help, to surface potential ministries and leaders, to inform them on the health of the congregation, and the like.

or informal membership). Also, participation in corporate gatherings like annual meetings (which involve each attendee's commitment to the next year's budget and plans), should be considered the obligation of each person.

The elder's first responsibilities are his leadership and teaching in his ministries: "those who diligently *labor* among you," (1 Thess. 5:12, italics added); "those who *led* you, who spoke the Word of God to you," (Heb. 13:7, italics added). This service fits him for his work on the elder council—making collective decisions for the congregation. Having considered biblical eldership and biblical governance by the elder council, we are now in a position to scrutinize this decision-making responsibility. How do the men of the elder council decide on the care of God's family? How do the elders come to agreement on His will for the church?

Lift up your eyes and look on the fields,
that they are white for harvest.
John 4:35

Chapter 5

Planning

PAUL REFERS TO THE EPHESIAN ELDERS AS OVERSEERS (Acts
20:28), who must guard themselves and the church.
Maintaining the biblical integrity of the council itself and the
congregation is one of the preeminent collective obligations of the
council. However, the task of guarding integrity is more
comprehensive than simply guaranteeing that doctrinal and moral
purity are preserved, and extends over more time than the here and
now. This work includes providing the body with forthcoming
opportunities for spiritual formation, fellowship, and worship, and,
above all, guaranteeing the church's dedicated responsiveness to
the Chief Shepherd's command, the Great Commission. The local
body must not be so absorbed with meeting its internal needs, and
dealing with day-to-day business, that it fails to conduct its part in
the expansion of the kingdom. We leaders must extend our
planning horizon out into the future as we map out a path for the
church.

Planning is the proactive aspect of elder oversight. Good
planning heads off many of the difficulties that fully occupy most
councils. Steering the church in the right direction is far better than
being occupied continuously in damage control.

Planning and monitoring of progress are among the most
important collective responsibilities of the council. That church will
be judged well led whose council makes today's decisions from
within the framework of both the church's properly evaluated history,
and a course for its future previously charted by its elders. Governing
the church in these times requires what is called strategic planning.
To some, this may seem another of those unbiblical intrusions from
the secular business world, or an unnecessary bureaucratic barrier to
getting on with the effort. But, in reality, all of us operate from a plan,
even if unwritten and unexamined. This is true, even if the intent is

merely to survive, maintain the status quo, or cope with situations as they occur.

In point of fact, proper planning involves the biblical concepts of setting a direction, prioritizing, and counting the cost. A competent shepherd would never set out with his flock without a plan to escort them to safety or to suitable pasture. As discussed previously, the elder's biblical role of ruling (*proïstēmi,* leading) means *leading by virtue of being out in front of those for whom we are responsible* (see p. 20). In order to lead collectively, all members of an elder council must be in agreement on the future direction of their church, and, with the rest of its leadership, be able to present effectively to the congregation a well-designed course. This collective vision casting is the type of planning process absolutely essential when an organization is led by a team. The essence of strategic planning is the leadership's choice "by consensus" of the church's future direction. Any leader who hesitates to engage in strategic planning must ask himself whether it is prudent to let the church drift aimlessly, or for him to proceed in any direction without the support of the rest of the leadership.

The essence of strategic planning is the leadership's choice "by consensus" of the church's future direction.

The purpose of strategic planning is to guide the church in understanding why it exists and what strategies it will adopt in the next three or four years to make a significant impact. It is the process of envisioning a proper biblical future for the church and seeing that its key leaders are taking the same heading as they work toward that future. Course-setting is only complete when all the council members can own, and are prepared to articulate, a scenario that has been formulated through their consensus.

In terms of facilitating teamwork and achieving shared goals, the planning process is more important than the plan itself. So strategic planning must involve all the major decision-makers in the church. The elder council that delegates planning to a senior pastor, church staff, or an elder committee (or attempts to copy a plan developed by another church), commits a serious blunder. The result will be a lack of ownership of the plan by the leadership, and ultimately the congregation.

Past experience with these top-down approaches has given strategic planning a negative reputation for some who have dealt with it in the corporate world. When strategic planning is conducted by management staff and then imposed on the personnel in the operating departments, such top-down planning can straightjacket the organization, stifle creativity, and even lead the business entity down the wrong path. To counter this misapplication of the method, it is vital that those who actually will be leading the work are the same people who are charged with the planning.

It is vital that those who actually will be leading the work are the same people who are charged with the planning.

However, this presents the dilemma cogently put by the Alliance for Non Profit Management: "Groups are great for many things, but writing is not one of them."[49] Therefore, the recommendation is that proposed ideas should be developed by the decision-makers, but the process of the narrowing down of the possibilities and the preparation of the written plan (subject to reviews), should be assigned to a small committee by the council.

The various elements of strategic planning and their logical flow are only briefly reviewed here. Excellent resources for nonprofit organizations, available in print and on the Internet,[50] apply to the church organization. Those responsible for spearheading the planning process in their church should avail themselves of these or similar resources to be in a position both to steer the process and instruct others in implementing the various steps. Or, the first time it prepares a strategic plan, the church may employ a consultant (who has a proven record) to guide and instruct it.

TERMINOLOGY

Strategic planning is not new. Many examples of it may be seen in the history of Israel and the church. Nehemiah's plan to return to Judah to restore Jerusalem is a prime example. Since the 1960s, strategic planning has become a standardized discipline taught in business schools. In the 1970s, variations in the methodology developed, with some redefinition of terms. However, neither of two of the most prominent, newer, alternative approaches is suitable for a church, since it is either reactive (the critical issues approach), or focuses on extending what the organization does best (the capabilities-based analysis), instead of on the church's God-given mandate. In this chapter, the classic, goal-driven methodology will be described, since this is the approach most commonly applied to nonprofits; and key terms are defined as they are most commonly employed in this type of strategic planning. Other definitions are perfectly acceptable as long as all involved understand and agree to use the same meanings. If a church does not use consistent terminology, leaders will become frustrated, even speaking at cross-purposes, spreading confusion.

The term "strategic" means "choosing how best to respond to the [expected future] circumstances."[51] It is applied to "plan" because strategic describes a technique that involves selecting the *optimum* approach in a *changing* environment. A strategic plan is not the same as an annual implementation plan, or even a long-term (multiyear) plan—both of which assume a fixed organization and known environment for the duration of the path chosen. These plans are the proper and necessary offspring of a strategic plan, but they are not themselves strategic. A strategic plan is designed to set overall direction and priorities that will be responsive to changes in the environment, including changes to the entity itself. It stops short of specifying the details that are found in an implementation plan. The strategic plan details *how* the church will make decisions (set priorities) that will accomplish its mission and lead it, over a specific period of time, into and through its chosen future. This requires good assessment, but not perfect knowledge, of the future. The strategic plan also formulates means of using change for the benefit of God's work.

The strategic plan formulates means of using change for the benefit of God's work.

All that has been said here is predicated on the assumption that the church in question is not in a holding pattern, but is striving to fulfill Christ's command to bring the Gospel to those both near and far. Too often we are focused inward, caught up in "doing church," and have lost the big picture, a redemptive perspective of the charge we received from Christ. Jesus told Peter, "I will *build* my church" (Matt. 16:18, italics added). Elders are not called to maintain or preserve the church, but to nurture and propagate her. If we do not share a sense of urgency about this task, we need to refocus, to reexamine the condition of those who live around us and the outcome for them if they do not become part of God's family.

To paraphrase James Belasco and Jarve Stead, authors of *Soaring With the Phoenix, not* to develop a strategic plan for our specific church is to embark on a journey over the uncharted seas "without a 'beacon' (vision), 'binoculars' (mission), or a 'compass' (values)."[52]

PLANNING

A strategic plan for a church includes the consideration of the following in the approximate order shown:

- The church's shared, core values

- The church's statement of its vision for its future: a visualization of the church and its ministries at the end of the plan period

- The church's mission statement: consisting of its purpose, endeavor, and shared values

- Assessment of the current internal environment of the church

- Assessment of the current and future external environment of the church

- Broad strategies to achieve the vision

- The church's goals: the pillars that support the vision

These steps then form the basis for creating an annual or operating plan for each year of the strategic plan. The annual plan will consist of time-phased objectives with their implementation tactics:

- Objectives: the measurable milestones that move the church toward its goals

- Tactics or techniques to achieve the church's goals, including a structure for deploying the resources for implementation

At first glance, this process appears linear—steps taken one after another, without ever retracing the path. However, focusing on one step in the process, without considering the consequences for those that follow, is unlikely. Also, revising a previous step is not unusual, either due to the effect it will have on the step currently being considered, or because of the wisdom gained as the leadership continues through the process.

Figure 1 illustrates the phasing of the steps and incorporated reviews of the initial steps. The starting positions—on both values and the vision statement—must pass the reality test of the assessment of the church's environment. It may be that the church's vision for ministry is entirely inadequate for the "fields that . . . are white for

PLANNING

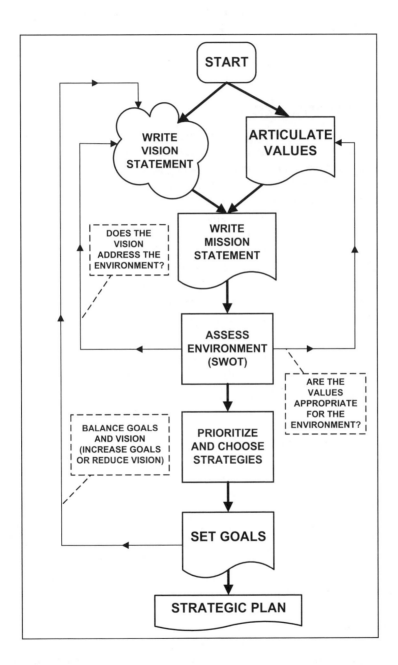

FIGURE 1 – THE STRATEGIC PLANNING PROCESS

harvest." At the end of the planning process, we must be sure that if we reach our goals, we will have secured the achievement of our vision. Either this, or the vision must be brought in line with what the church believes are the maximum goals for which it can strive.

SHARED VALUES

The first task of strategic planning is to *identify* the core beliefs or values that will guide the church in the pursuit of its vision. In most cases, these values are already present, having helped to shape the church's vision. These standards should be sufficiently defined to differentiate the church in question from other churches and institutions, and to adequately shape the church's present and future decisions. For example, belief in God, prayer, worship, and loving others are core convictions so generic that they cannot even distinguish the body under consideration from some cults. Better examples are prizing belief in the God revealed in the Old and New Testaments, practicing individual and corporate prayer to prompt supernatural intervention, promoting authentic worship that expresses the heart, and demonstrating Christ-like love for our neighbors.

The church's stated values will be the most important component of the church's strategic plan.

The church's stated values will be the most important component of the church's strategic plan. A simple example illustrates this truth. Which is more important in determining the future conduct of a young person leaving home for college? The plans discussed ahead of time with his parents, or the student's core values?

To test the adequacy of their stated chosen values, the elders should ask themselves whether they will be satisfied with any shape the church takes ten years from now, just as long as that form continues to display the chosen values. This adequacy test runs counter to the often-expressed double intention: to be exact and brief. We want to express our values concisely so they are easy for the congregation to remember, and are value statements short enough to fit into the church's mission statement. (The mission statement is intended to communicate the church's purpose to the congregation and the outside world). But that brevity may lead to unacceptable imprecision. The conflicting needs for precision and simplicity can be met by short summary phrases for each value, with accompanying longer explanations.

VISION STATEMENT

According to the Alliance for Non Profit Management, "There is one universal rule of planning: You will never be greater than the vision that guides you."[53] A strategy must lead somewhere, so, parallel with the establishment of values, the elders should be prayerfully developing a vision for the church's future.

A vision statement describes the future desired destination, the specific target: what the church will be (internal vision) and its effect on the community (external vision) at the completion of the plan. Experts on planning for nonprofits recommend that this span not exceed five years, three being the preferred period. Therefore, strategic planning must be dynamic, and be updated every several years, with each new planning horizon set within the easily foreseeable future.

DEFINITION

Michael Allison and Jude Kaye of the Support Center for Nonprofit Management provide a useful definition: "A vision is a guiding image of success. If a mission statement provides a blueprint for the organization's work—the what, why, and how of what it does—then the vision is the artist's rendering of the realization of that mission."[54] These authorities on strategic planning add: "The challenge is to create a vision that is grand enough to inspire people, but also . . . that is grounded in sufficient reality that people can start to believe that it can and will happen."[55]

Though most experts in this field advocate using this definition of vision, many church leaders disagree. The approach of Randy Pope, senior pastor of Perimeter Church in suburban Atlanta, is typical of many church leaders: "The vision of a prevailing church will be broad and long enough to encompass whatever time remains in history. . . . A vision ought to be open-ended."[56] Strategic planner Carter MacNamara objects to this kind of statement, saying that many organizations thereby have reduced the vision statement to "a motivational tool, too often including highly idealistic phrasing and activities to which the organization cannot realistically aspire."[57]

Other leaders try to formulate a vision statement that will be a fixed unchangeable beacon for the church as it proceeds into its future, however far away that may extend. For several reasons, this is a naive and unworkable approach. The vision must change as the horizon shifts. A church plant may begin with a vision of establishing itself as a self-supporting church, but, once this vision has been reached, the church requires a new vision to prevent stagnation. For instance, a major population change must energize the church to either relocate with the population, or alter its vision to focus on the needs of the new population. Attempts to design a vision statement so broadly that it can withstand any variation will have at least two consequences: progress toward that vision can never be measured, and the particular church's vision will be indistinguishable from those of other evangelical bodies.

Without our team's goal line in view, we will be evaluating ourselves merely on plays executed, instead of on the yardage gained.

The vision statement defines our team's goal line on the playing field. Without that goal line in view, we will be evaluating ourselves merely on plays executed, instead of on the yardage gained toward our goal.

CREATING A VISION STATEMENT

No doubt the creation of a vision is the most daunting task of all, since it requires a conceptual grasp of an advantageous future for the church that is clearly informed by a biblical view of how the Gospel may be presented to the changing culture in the church's community. A vision statement is a picture of what the church and its ministries will or should look like at the end of the period covered by the proposed plan, and how the church will be serving the congregation and achieving its outreach to the community. An effective vision statement must be:

- Concise, easily understood. "If the bugle produces an indistinct sound, who will prepare himself for battle?" (1 Cor. 14:8)

- Descriptive of a future that is clearly discernable from the present. "What will success look like?"[58]

- Credible

- Worthy of Christ's church

- Specific to your church and different from those of neighboring churches

- Ambitious, setting a high standard, requiring faith

- Motivating, inspiring commitment

A vision statement paints a picture of a destination that is not the church's ultimate target, but a way station on its church's journey. To be an adequate statement, it must be clear that the church is not presently at the desired place. It must envision a future condition that may be difficult but is possible to achieve. The vision statement that describes the current situation, states the obvious, does not require change, or is otherwise vague, is clearly unacceptable. The statement—"The church projects a future in which it has an effect on the community for Christ"—is not quantifiable or unique, and could apply to any local evangelical body. An effective vision statement requires clear descriptions, carefully delineated, in order to differentiate the particular body from neighboring churches.

A vision statement is a picture of what the church and its ministries will or should look like at the end of the period covered by the proposed plan.

On the other hand, a description of an outcome that either is impossible, or cannot be reached in the time frame selected, will not motivate God's people or focus the direction of their church: "The church envisions a future when all the residents of the community honor Christ." If the congregation cannot imagine a plausible mental picture of the desired future state, the vision statement is impotent.

As part of its strategic plan, a group designing a church plant could offer this vision statement: "Our vision is a new evangelical church that will serve the eastern suburbs, and that, within three years, will be self-governing, self-sustaining, and offering ministries for all age groups."

A familiar example of a solid vision statement is President John F. Kennedy's "This nation should commit itself to achieving the goal, before this decade is out, of landing a man on the moon and returning him safely to the earth" (1961).[59] This assertion had all the characteristics of an effective vision statement; It was clear, concise, audacious—but credible—and the country was motivated to embark on a great and ultimately successful effort.

Paul painted a vivid vision (without a stated timetable) of the final triumph of the kingdom by quoting Isaiah: "For we will all stand before God's judgment seat. It is written: 'As surely as I live, says the

Lord, every knee shall bow before me; every tongue will confess to God'" (Rom. 14:10–11, *NIV*).

Fine-tuned creativity is requisite when writing a vision statement for an established church's prospects. Properly so, we are reluctant to apply standards common in the business world, such as numerical growth, competitive position, and so forth. However, the statement can point to measurable improvement in, and expansions of, the church's ministries and influence on the served community.

STIMULATING THE PROCESS

Business experts James Kouzes and Barry Posner say studies teach us that the leader who can accurately and realistically evaluate his past is better able to visualize and understand his future.

> It appears that when we gaze first into our past, we elongate our future. We also enrich our future and give it detail as we recall the richness of our experiences. In other words, reflecting upon our past may enhance our ability to be forward-looking. . . . None of this is to say that our past is our future. Adopting that extremely dangerous perspective would be not unlike trying to drive to our future while looking only in the rearview mirror. . . . [However], leaders would be well advised to avail themselves of the richest set of experiences possible. The broader their experiences and the vaster their network of connections, the longer their time horizons are likely to be.[60]

Therefore, a thorough review of its own church history, of the legacy of the church at large, and of the implications of current movements in evangelicalism will greatly assist an elder council in formulating its vision for the future of its own church.

One way to stimulate the creation of a vision statement is for the full council to examine the projected, future external environment, and brainstorm possible ways the church could have an effect. A select group could then be assigned to refine and choose several of the most promising vision statements. This group should be comprised of men who are creative, analytical, and able to think abstractly. Next, before the full council, each offering is evaluated against the others for its compatibility with the church's mission, values, the community's needs, and financial realism. Why the smaller designated committee? If the council has more than seven members, like most large committees, it will probably seek the lowest common denominator,[61] meaning the one formulation no one disagrees with, and the church will be saddled with an insipid vision statement.

MISSION STATEMENT

The intent of the church's mission statement is to communicate clearly and succinctly to both members and onlookers *why* the church exists and *what* its work is. This declaration should motivate people to become involved with the church. The mission statement is not part of the strategic plan. Rather, it is a critical communication tool. A mission statement normally combines four elements:

- The **purpose**, or why the church exists and what it is seeking to accomplish

- The **main methods** to be used in achieving the church's purpose

- The **scope** of the church's activities

- The **values** that guide the church in pursuing its purpose

When we first take a look, distinguishing purpose from vision may appear difficult. The key to understanding is realizing the difference in perspective. The **purpose** describes *why* the church exists and *what* it seeks to accomplish, while the **vision statement** gives an image in words of what success will look like when realized. An example of a viable mission statement is:

Our mission is to become an authentic biblical community [values] that invites people to meet the living Jesus Christ, that nurtures and equips [method] them to serve Him and one another, and that plants and serves other churches [purpose] in our greater area and throughout the world [scope].

Notice the infinitive "to become." This shows an intent to make a change, which should be a salient characteristic of all mission statements.

SWOT ANALYSIS

The two aspects of environmental assessment are often combined under the term, SWOT analysis, an acronym in common parlance for assessing **S**trengths, **W**eaknesses, **O**pportunities, and **T**hreats. Strengths and weaknesses define the internal environment of the church; opportunities and threats evaluate the external milieu. The internal analysis examines the church's leadership, programs, services, resources (people and finances), and organizational effectiveness. The external analysis studies the current and future opportunities and obstacles for ministry outside the church.

The SWOT analysis may, and probably should, occasion a review of the vision statement. These tasks must be undertaken interactively. Evaluation of the external environment (need for the Gospel in the church's area of influence), and the internal environment (the Lord's past and current blessing of the church's ministries) will strongly influence the composition of the vision. The leadership cannot complete conceptualizing their vision for their church without weighing the needs of the neighborhood (and the world), and reflecting on God's specific guidance up to this point in its history. The mission statement also properly narrows the scope of the SWOT. Many community needs—for instance, for better transportation—will not qualify for consideration in the SWOT analysis, since they are irrelevant to the achievement of the church's vision. This is also true of threats. For example, the fact that a local ordinance requires that union members do all construction work will not be of significance if refurbishing low-income housing is not part of the church's vision.

Many have found the work done by Christian Schwarz, *Natural Church Development*,[62] very helpful in assessing the internal strengths and weaknesses of one's church. This researcher has developed the thesis that people are reached and accompanying growth occurs naturally wherever high quality is present in the church. Schwarz conducted an empirical research project in one thousand churches in thirty-two countries and identified the following eight distinct quality factors:

- Empowering leadership: The leadership concentrates on empowering other Christians for service.

- Gift-oriented ministry: The congregants are encouraged to serve in their areas of giftedness.

PLANNING

- Passionate spirituality: Prayer in the church is inspiring.

- Functional structures: The church has an effective and helpful organizational structure.

- Inspiring worship service: In its services, people connect with God.

- Holistic small groups: Its groups apply concepts derived from Bible study to their lives.

- Need-oriented evangelism: Its evangelism speaks to the perceived needs of non-Christians.

- Loving relationships: A high degree of community is present over and beyond that created by scheduled events.[63]

In the United States, surveys based on this research may be obtained from ChurchSmart Resources and given to a representative sample of a church's leadership. Such a survey will determine how that church scores in each category, compared with worldwide averages.[64] ChurchSmart Resources will process the completed surveys and provide graphs and interpretations of the results.

The external study—of the current and future external environments of the church—investigates the population within range of the church, with its changing demographic attributes, generational changes, and general worldview. George Barna spells out the latter to include: "key attitudes they possess, the values that determine their thoughts and lifestyle, the beliefs that shape their character, the lifestyles that describe their daily activities, and the felt needs they possess."[65]

The most difficult information to capture is a thorough understanding of the values and interests of the unchurched.

Data obtained from local governments, school districts, newspapers, and realtors are useful in completing the external analysis. The most difficult information to capture is a thorough understanding of the values and interests of the unchurched, since many of us are socially isolated from them. However, this information is vital and can be

113

obtained from national polling results,[66] supplemented by local canvasses taken by your church.

To predict the future we must carefully extrapolate observable past and current changes into the future, for the duration of the strategic plan. Threats arise from cultural change and overt opposition. Because only a small percentage of residents in most communities attend evangelical churches, saturation of the community by other churches is not a threat. Rivalry is not from other churches, but a force emanating from our workplaces, children's sports leagues, professional and social associations, and the like. The competition issues directly, and especially, from our standard of living choices and the value system promulgated by society (with significant assistance from the media). However, understanding those programs and assets being offered by your neighboring churches and their degree of success in advancing the kingdom will add to your understanding of the external environment. Such an evaluation should also expose those community needs that could be met—but are not being met—by its churches, and the reasons the vast majority of the local population has not been reached, or has not responded.

To illustrate the typical elements, below is a simplified version of a SWOT analysis generated by a church:

Strengths:
- Growing congregation
- Worship and praise service attractive to visitors
- Sunday School's positive reputation
- Vigorous women's ministry

Opportunities:
- New families moving into community
- Parents' concerns about junior and senior high youth
- Youth's interest in athletics and social events

Weaknesses:
- Inadequate facilities
- Insufficient number of leaders
- Debt load from mortgage
- No significant youth ministry

Threats:
- Hostility of zoning authorities to facility expansion
- Pressures of workplaces on leaders
- Employment relocations of present leaders

The SWOT analysis is an advantageous method of involving broad-based participation in the strategic planning process. The results of the analysis of the external environment should be supplied to all church ministries to support their own SWOT studies. After each ministry team has analyzed its own situation, the elders may use the collated results in formulating a high-level, church-wide assessment.

STRATEGIES

Planners use the term "strategy" to refer to a *broad* approach for achieving the future state described in a vision statement, and it will be used here in this sense. The word "strategy" is also being used by other planners to refer to the tactics needed to achieve each individual objective, these tactics obviously also being strategies. But, to avoid confusion, the term "tactics" will be employed herein to refer to the specific approaches required to achieve the individual objectives, as opposed to the term "strategy," which will be reserved for the broad method.

Once there is a definite target vision and the church's purpose has been clarified, the time has come to rank the programs and activities that will accomplish the vision. Strategies define the means the church will be using to address its identified opportunities and threats, by exploiting its strengths and correcting its weaknesses (SWOT analysis), all within the framework of its available resources. Strengths that match identified needs (opportunities in the external community) are especially noteworthy, and deserve priority in the strategy. If the church was a business attempting to maximize its profits, it would divest itself of, or de-emphasize, ministry in its areas of weakness. However, the church is about the Lord's business, so some areas that are weak may be crucial to accomplishing God's work for the church, and, therefore, merit preference for strengthening. For instance, a church weak in evangelism must consider correcting this flaw a high priority.

> **Strengths that match identified needs—**
> **opportunities in the external community**
> **—deserve priority in the strategy.**

The first step in developing a strategy is a careful examination of current activities and programs. Are they congruent with the church's mission? Are they effective? What start-ups should be proposed? Bear in mind that anything new must compete with present programs for available resources, or be paid for by increased investment. An aggressive strategy will include some fresh initiatives, and probably divestment of some existing activities. As the church moves into the second and third years of its strategic plan, and if the plan involves outreach, numerical growth resulting from the right choices in the first year should finance additional initiatives in the successive years.

Although the SWOT analysis is helpful in guiding the strategy formation process, it cannot be systematized. No substitutes exist for discussion, prayer, and tapping the wisdom of creative brothers and sisters in the church. Obviously, the resulting strategies must be broad enough to allow for future emerging concepts to be considered during the life of the plan and not suppressed because they are viewed as being "outside the plan." The church that locks itself into a narrow plan could miss a major opportunity for effective ministry. The purpose of planning is to assure progress on goals, not to stifle creativity.[*]

Tragically, most strategic planning efforts end right here! Except for the possibility that the vision, values, and mission positions taken by a church may appear in some of its publications, the plan is filed away, out of mind, not used. Consequently, the next time anyone attempts to engage the leadership in planning, he will meet great resistance and skepticism, because the last effort apparently had all the merit of a mere exercise. If any vision is to be realized, the overall strategic plan must be converted to goals and measurable objectives, with associated practical tactics to accomplish each.

GOALS

Strategies result in planned outcomes called goals. According to George Barna, "A vision that has no goals and plans associated with it is merely a fantasy. A team without goals and plans is merely a social club."[68] Goals break down or convert the "what" of the church's purpose into a set or list of qualitative outcomes that, taken together, will assure the achievement of its vision. The goals are the pillars that support the vision. If properly defined, their subsequent achievement accomplishes the vision.

Referring back to the vision statement of the group planning a church plant, their stated three-year purpose (of being established as

---

[*] Henry Mintzberg, author of *The Rise and Fall of Strategic Planning: Reconceiving Roles for Planning, Plans, Planners*, provides a useful analysis of the excesses of strategic planning as practiced by the staffs of corporations.[67]

an independent church) could be divided into the necessary supporting components: for instance, the creation of a worship and praise team, a preaching-teaching team, a graded children's program, an adult education program, an elder council, a deacon ministry, sufficient stewardship to support the church, permanent facilities, and so forth.

"A vision that has no goals and plans associated with it is merely a fantasy." *George Barna*

Goals, and their related objectives and the subsequent tactics (to be defined below), must be delineated by those who will be held accountable for fulfilling them, in consultation with the elder council. In this way, these leaders take a proprietary interest in their own pieces of the responsibility, and the goals serve as challenges that require their response and movement.

OBJECTIVES

Planners differ about whether time-phased, quantifiable objectives should be part of the strategic plan or left to the resulting implementation plans, but the latter course is preferred. At this point, we move out of strategic planning and into the implementation plan, or annual operating plan. Since it is of short duration (typically one year), this plan, as distinguished from a strategic plan, can assume a known environment and a fixed, church organizational structure. Compared with multiyear goals, objectives are quantitative. It is at this juncture that the individual members of the ministry teams, the church leaders, go on record as to their specific intentions for making progress toward the chosen future. If the strategic plan was for three years, these annual plan commitments should take the church approximately one-third of the way toward the end stated in the vision statement.

The annual plan should be broken down or organized in the same manner as the strategic plan, so that the two correlate. In both plans, the strategic plan goals will be listed, connecting the two plans. The projected outcome of the strategic plan (the goals) will never be obtained unless this step of defining the objectives is taken. Objectives are identical to action steps. However, some use the term "action steps" to indicate those stretch goals an organization agrees to work toward to improve its performance. But, as it is the preference of most planners, the term "objectives" will be used to avoid confusion. Objectives are defined as those concrete accomplishments, the fulfillment of which moves the church a measurable distance toward securing its vision.

Each goal or sub-goal from the strategic plan will have a corresponding objective. Goals that require multiple objectives for their definition should be subdivided into sub-goals. Properly stated objectives are:

- Action-oriented: Each starts with the infinitive verb "to," followed by an action verb.

- Specific: Each defines the exact outcome.

- Time-limited: Each has specific start and stop dates.

- Realistic: Each is believed to be achievable, and capable of being completed in the specified time.

TACTICS

Tactics are the means by which each objective will be realized. Without tactics, the realism of the plan, and, especially, the accompanying budget, cannot be assessed. In addition, tactics explain the approaches the team members will be using during the time segment chosen (usually one year) to minister to those in their charge.

In the case of our example, the church plant, the alignment of one of its goals with its corresponding objective and tactic might be:

- **Strategic goal:** to provide top-quality Sunday School classes for all grade-school children

- **First-year objective:** to provide independent classroom space and a three-person teaching team for each two-grade combination (first and second, third and fourth, fifth and sixth grades)

- **Tactic:** provide three classrooms, recruit and train three lead and six assistant teachers, and select and purchase graded curriculum

Whenever funds are required for its implementation, each objective or action step must be tied to a budget entry. An unfunded objective will only be a source of frustration for the team—an untenable juxtaposition which amounts to intentional sabotage! Leaders will simply withdraw their participation in future planning. This is not to say that objectives should never be redesigned so they will require less funding or fit a given budget. Objectives may have to be eliminated altogether because of limited funds. Available workers and financial resources must be prudently allocated to individual objectives if the church is to progress toward its vision.

Tying the annual plan to the goals of the strategic plan is crucial. Too often, an annual plan only allocates the resources necessary to perform ministry. It does not define the corresponding, expected ministry accomplishments, and, thereby, fails to provide for accountability. For instance, a youth department budget may show its staffing level, and the events and activities planned for the coming year, but this does not commit the staff and volunteers of the youth department to accomplish anything. Achievements (especially incremental attainments over the past year) must be measured: the number of church youth involved, their friends brought to events, those incorporated into accountability Bible studies, the volunteer leaders trained, and so forth.

Tying the annual plan to the goals of the strategic plan is crucial.

The objectives are *not* the annual plan, but are that part of the plan that documents the intended incremental improvements beyond the previous year. Churches do not burden themselves with the accounting tedium of allocating labor (salaries of staff) to individual objectives, as is the practice in industry. Consequently, a ministry plan will simply state the staffing levels and expenses for the total of its ongoing programs for the year, and will justify the appropriateness of its staffing levels according to the planned ministry activities.

New undertakings cannot be evaluated except in the context of a ministry's total annual plan, which shows all the activities and programs and their corresponding funding. (New undertakings are not always new ventures built on top of existing pursuits, but may be the reforming of past practices, or the replacements for discontinued projects.) When resources are limited, and they usually are, we must be prepared to discard time-honored programs that do not contribute to achieving the vision the Lord has brought to our attention.

Because the strategic planning process described here has been broken down into its parts, the method may seem paper intensive. In reality, this is not so. The annual plan for a ministry can be several sheets of paper that list each strategic sub-goal, with its related objective, tactic, a time frame, and responsible leader. An example is given in Figure 2. Numbering the sub-goals, or repeating them by name in the budget, correlates the budget to the annual plan.

MINISTRY_____

STRATEGIC PLAN GOAL_____

SUB-GOAL#:_____

SUB-GOAL_____

CURRENT YEAR OBJECTIVE_____

_____

TACTIC_____

_____

TIME SPAN   START | | | | | | |

           COMPLETION | | | | | | |

RESPONSIBLE LEADER_____

- -

MINISTRY_____

STRATEGIC PLAN GOAL_____

SUB-GOAL#:_____

SUB-GOAL_____

CURRENT YEAR OBJECTIVE_____

_____

TACTIC_____

_____

TIME SPAN   START | | | | | | |

           COMPLETION | | | | | | |

RESPONSIBLE LEADER_____

FIGURE 2 – ANNUAL PLAN FORMAT

REPORTING AND ACCOUNTABILITY

No doubt about it, accountability is both crucial and difficult in a primarily volunteer organization. However, when plans are in place in team ministry, accountability—because it can be built into the system —is enhanced. Given that each ministry team has committed to carry out a certain part of the church's overall ministry, each team leader must shepherd his team in fulfilling its planned objectives. Or else he must come back to the elders, far in advance of each review date, to ask for help in the form of guidance, additional resources, or (worst case) reformulating authority. In a team-based organization, it is unacceptable for a team leader to arrive at a review point and surprise the others with the fact that their team will not meet its part of the overall plan. With the discipline of time-phased objectives, providing periodic progress reports to the council is eased for ministry teams.

Accountability also produces the feedback elders need so that they can adequately recognize ministry participants for their specific accomplishments. Wherever we rely heavily on volunteers, appreciation and recognition are vital in motivating and encouraging them.

THE PLANNING CYCLE

Strategic planning is not a one-time event; it never ends. If a three-year cycle is chosen, prior to its first year the strategic plan and the first year's annual plan are developed. For the second and third years, new annual plans are set up. Before the end of the third year, a new three-year strategic plan is prepared—this time a much less daunting task since the major directional decisions were made initially. But, at that point, reviewing the church's experience in traveling its chosen path and the realism of its original vision is appropriate. As the next strategic plan is prepared, some course corrections may be in order, as the Lord clarifies and enlarges the elders' vision for the church.

AN IMPORTANT CAUTION

Planning can be a great blessing to the church, but it is not without dangers. The most egregious errors perverting strategic planning and, therefore, to be avoided, are:

PLANNING

- The attempt to drive a church with a plan: substituting planning for personal leadership, the failure of the elders to be out in front, leading the congregation

- Top-down planning: the failure to involve the ministry leadership in the formation of the plan

- The effort to sell the plan to leadership who were not involved in its creation

- Loose adherence to the church's values

- Rigid adherence to implementation tactics at the expense of creativity

It is my contention that elders and leaders have a spiritual obligation to properly shepherd the congregation by being proactive, rather than reactive. This is my reason for spending quite a bit of time here on the elder council's collective responsibility for planning.

Be devoted to one another in brotherly love,
give preference to one another in honor.
Romans 12:10

Chapter 6

Council Decisions

A COUNCIL MEETING, especially if it is referred to as an "Elder Board Meeting," calls up various images, depending on one's firsthand experience. Some people lack any exposure to elder governance, that is, church government by a body of elders. Consequently, they will not be aware of all that is entailed in elders' meetings. Or, they may assume that these sessions are equivalent to whatever it is that enables the ruling body of their church to manage its business. For others, even those familiar with an elder-governed church, the recollection or anticipation of taking part in council meetings may be distasteful, not an uplifting prospect. Though men acknowledge theoretically that elder governance is biblical, they find the requisite meetings tiresome, frustratingly inefficient, even secular when you come right down to it. And this has an even wider effect, for an elder's lack of both enthusiasm and sense of accomplishment infects his family with resentment of the time he spends away from them.

Depending on the source—a member of the paid staff, an elder, or the ordinary church attendee—the following complaints about elder councils and their meetings are often voiced:

- Inadequate time is devoted to worship, prayer, and fellowship.

- Meetings are tedious, boring, poorly conducted, and exasperating.

- Meetings are devoted to the administration of the church rather than to overall ministry goals and reporting.

- The council does not know what is really going on.

- Meetings are irrelevant to the ministries of the church since the council elders are not personally involved in those ministries.

- Since all major decisions are made outside the meetings anyway, by the senior staff, the council meetings are unrelated to the functioning of the church, so, "There is nothing important on the agenda."

- The elders get together merely to "rubber stamp" what the professional staff or the council chairman has already decided.

- The elders are intrusive "armchair" directors who butt into the business, and second-guess the determinations, of the paid staff.

- Meetings consume too much time, time better spent in actual ministry effort or with family. It takes too long to achieve results.

- Agendas are so taken up with current business and trivial detail that elders do not plan for the future.

- Meetings are disorganized, not kept on track or focused, and the participants, who do not arrive prepared well, are undisciplined.

However, a growing number of churches are discovering that when the decision process used in council meetings is biblical and wise, elder council meetings can be highly productive and a positive experience for those involved. Amazing transformation in the character of meetings takes place when the council's behavior changes from critiquing the work of the staff, to brothers sharing from personal experience what God has been doing in their ministries, and to seeking their fellow elders' counsel and prayers.

MAKING DECISIONS

Church leadership by the elder council, commissions, committees, and leadership team involves making decisions for God's people. At the outset, we need to deal with two practices which set the limits on how outcomes are determined: either achieving the simple majority vote of those present in a meeting, or requiring their unanimous vote. But is either of these the best way for a council to find the mind of Christ for His church?

UNANIMITY OR MAJORITY RULE?

Both the Old and New Testaments consistently teach the necessity and benefit of unity. "Behold, how good and how pleasant it is for brothers to dwell together in unity!" (Ps. 133:1). In His High Priestly Prayer, Jesus asked the Father that His disciples would "be perfected in unity, so that the world may know that You sent Me" (John 17:23). Paul pressed the brothers: "Now I exhort you, brethren, by the name of our Lord Jesus Christ, that you all agree and there be no divisions among you, but that you be made complete in the same mind and in the same judgment" (1 Cor. 1:10). Be "diligent to preserve the unity of the Spirit in the bond of peace" (Eph. 4:3). "Beyond all these things put on love, which is the perfect bond of unity" (Col. 3:14).

But what does unity imply? Does it mean that every elder on the council will hold the same opinion? Does it suggest that if each elder was asked to submit his thoughts on a given issue, the notions of all would be uniform? No, for if this were the case, there would be no necessity for the plurality of elders.

Being unified on an issue or policy signifies that, after debate, discussion, and prayer, *all* the elders can support a certain choice as the best possible collective decision—the determination that has taken into account the well-being of the church and the concerns of *all* the elders. Because we have different histories, gifts, and personalities, unity on an elder council requires the hard work of applying Christian virtues, namely, "Be devoted to one another in brotherly love; give preference to one another in honor" (Rom. 12:10). Biblically, unity depends on humility (Eph. 4:2; Phil. 2:1–5). Making elder council decisions is an active exercise in corporate (that is, of the entire group) or collegiate (collectively considered) decision-making. No individual elder has the right to insist on his own opinion but must contribute the benefit of his own gifts to a wise decision reached by the whole council.

To assure unity, some churches require unanimous consent on all elders' decisions. Their councils will not proceed on a disputed matter until solidarity can be achieved. Churches with elder councils composed of godly men who have learned to work together well over a considerable period have successfully carried out this policy. They deliberately pray and wait until each man comes to the same conclusion. But this policy becomes more difficult as a council increases either in size, or experiences turnover due to resignations or a rotation policy. Every time a new man is added to the elder council, there is a period of learning for him and of adjustment for the others.

However, two potentialities militate against the wisdom of asserting the requirement of unanimity, especially in councils with more than a few men. First, and inadvertently, this practice fails to safeguard the church against a "savage wolf" arising from within the elders' ranks, since any *one* elder can shut down the decision-making process of the council. Regrettably, the choice to require unanimous consent on all decisions is also the decision to allow any individual elder to block the council from taking action to protect God's people. Even if we are very careful in appointing elders, the risk remains that one or more may be motivated by self-interest (Acts 20:29). Unanimity is a goal to be sought, but legislating it converts the search for the unanimity of the whole into the tyranny of an individual. Not taking an action is a decision. Granting one council member the privilege of making a unilateral choice violates the required principle that all decisions are to be made by a plurality of elders.

Legislating it converts the search for the unanimity of the whole into the tyranny of an individual.

Unwisely, many of us believe that a crisis originating from one "wolf," or even a pack of "wolves," will never occur in our churches. The early church experienced many such attacks, and Paul was explicit in urging vigilant attention to the *fact* that it will happen again (Acts 20:29–31). Church history is strewn with confirmation of his prophecy. Such a crisis is likely when an elder or pastor will not accept the appropriate discipline for a moral failing, or attempts to lead the church away from its roots out of personal self-interest. In such a case, some elders are likely to support a popular leader, to the detriment, even the splitting, of the church.

These tough issues, in which unanimity is extremely difficult, often lead to a breakdown in the council's protection of the congregation. Sadly, almost a third of the churches in the United States have experienced the moral failure of a leader. Such leaders have usually built close relationships with some of the elders. When a crisis caused by the guilty party's failure occurs, his close friends on the council will be willing to jeopardize the safety of the congregation and the purity of the church in the desire to show mercy to their friend, and the other men may go along for the sake of unanimity.

Secondly, deadlock will stymie that elder council that requires unanimity for its decisions. And over issues of far less consequence than that of a wolf springing up in its midst. All it takes is one elder who takes a stand against a certain idea or plan (perhaps by virtue of his personal history), and the council is obstructed. This is not to say that the objection of one man, because he is in the minority, is to be disregarded. His point of view should occasion serious review of the impending decision. However, the council is charged with the protection and ongoing health of the flock, and must avoid nurturing what may be merely the idiosyncrasy of one member. For instance, a bias in favor of the status quo is harmful to a church, especially when its challenges are ever-changing.

Some churches are passionate and resolute about requiring unanimity on every elder council decision, and report occasions on which observing this procedure saved them from making unwise decisions. Paul Winslow and Dorman Followwill, in their work documenting Peninsula Bible Church's experience, detail several examples.[69] However, it is unwise to base policy on anecdotal evidence from a limited experience base. Interestingly, Doug Goins, one of the elders responsible for preaching at PBC, observes that, in order to maintain this policy, it has proved necessary to remove some elders from PBC's council because they were "contrary, obstructionist, and inflexible."[70] In other words, some elders consistently prevented the achievement of unanimity.

This concern is not so much of an issue for groups subordinate to the council which may contain personnel other than elders. Unity is also important in these bodies, but, because they function under the authority of the council, they have the option of referring a decision to the council when full agreement cannot be reached.

A decision achieved by only a slim majority of the elders leaves the council divided and unable to lead.

The opposite extreme, the practice of requiring the approval of only a majority of the elders to decide a matter, is even more deficient. The elders are not only responsible for directing the congregation but for leading it. A decision achieved by only a slim majority of the elders leaves the council divided and unable to lead. A proposal that cannot gain the concurrence of all or nearly all of the elders is not worthy of the elders' support. How can the elders expect the flock to follow if they themselves cannot unite? Elder decisions are collective or collegiate decisions; it is essential that the council work together to reach the best corporate decisions.

CONSENSUS

There is a third option, another method of decision-making for the council, that of requiring *consensus, an opinion held by all or most.* The achievement of decisions by consensus is a middle ground between insisting on unanimity and accepting a bare majority vote. In fact, this middle ground is very close to unanimity. Unlike quick agreement or resolution of an issue by voting, arriving at consensus takes hard work. It does not require stifling of contrary opinions or conflict, or prevent healthy disagreement and debate. The process involves the back-and-forth discussion of the viewpoints of each and all—accompanied by prayer for the discernment of God's will—until there is general concurrence that all the issues have been considered. Consensus is finally achieved when all (or almost all) elders agree that a particular determination is the best decision that the council can make for the good of the church. Such a resolution may differ somewhat from the judgment each elder might prefer if he alone was to decide the matter, but it is a judgment which all or nearly all of the elders can support.

Consensus: an opinion held by all or most.

The council moderator should remind the elders that their task is not to vote issues up or down but to find the will of Christ on each. To do this, they must strive for solutions all can support, rather than settle for those choices that garner the most votes. When the matter is not time-critical, members should feel free to request a delay, an interval for more prayer and creative thinking, so a resolution that all can fully support may be crafted. This result is predicated on the practice of encouraging dissenting brothers to explain fully their hesitation. The other council elders will need to respect the conscientious objection of that brother who is uncertain of the merits of a proposed resolution. At the same time, each council member must accept the discipline of seeking the best collective decisions, rather than the ruling closest to his personal preference.

One useful method of encouraging unanimity in decisions, while remaining elastic in case the Lord intends another perspective, is the adoption of the following procedure: if any *two* elders agree that the resolution approved by the council presents the risk of going against Christ's will for the church that is *greater* than the risk of delay to the health of the flock, they have the right to require delay and reconsideration at the next meeting. In the interim, all concerned are to pray about the matter and seek the Lord's guidance as to the advisability of the choice, or of modifying it sufficiently to accommodate the concerns of the dissenting brothers. The council must then decide if it is important to move forward even if two of its members continue to dissent from the decision. This policy shields the congregation from a precipitous, unwise decision made by a simple majority of the council. On the other hand, this policy prevents minority rule. Many of us can report that deferring initially to the two dissenting elders has almost always resulted in a better final determination. Godly elders will be very reluctant to act, even after delaying, if two members are unwilling to support the action. However, the council must preserve the right to go forward to protect the congregation, particularly in a time-critical situation.

Why require, in order to delay, that at least *two elders*—rather than a single man—be in agreement that the majority's choice is not acceptable (for them at that time)? Because it is reasonable that, if the concerns of one elder have sufficient merit, he should be able to gain the support of at least one more elder who agrees that his concern is significant enough to warrant a delay. Moreover, Christ gave weight to the agreement of two: "If two of you agree on earth about anything that they may ask, it shall be done for them" (Matt. 18:19). The requirement that two concur before postponement assures that the objection is more substantive than the mere preference of one elder.

Finding consensus as to Christ's best for the church requires concerted effort. If we elders merely settle on the lowest common denominator to achieve decisions by consensus, we are not fulfilling our duty to the Head of the church or to the specific congregation we are charged with leading and governing.

THREATS TO DECIDING BY CONSENSUS

The gold standard for elder council decisions is that they be biblical, wise, and beneficial agreements by consensus that all its members will support. Decisions born of prayer, accurate information, full study, and the meeting of godly minds will be favored with the greatest possible prospects for success.

This noble principle of elders ruling by consensus is constantly threatened, if not in danger of being literally lost along the way. We need to be candid in our evaluation of the situation. Continually, the council is under siege from its members' personal sin and character flaws, not the least of which is pride. Recognition that personal and corporate pride is an ever-present obstacle is the first step in dealing directly with it, and ripping off pride's many masks is the next. In either case, the chief obstacle is lack of elders' corporate prayer. The independence we (and our culture) prize leads us to habitually sidestep this imperative.

LACK OF PRAYER

In order to arrive at a consensus, each man on the elder council must be willing to set aside his own preferences and listen to the leading of the Holy Spirit. Obviously, we come to meetings from different previous church backgrounds, temperaments, and (in most cases) experience in our employment. Why is it so difficult to bear in mind the effect—and the purpose—of these influences? How can Christ's supernatural intervention be displayed through the leadership of such finite, flawed men? Beyond that, how can men with such differences exhibit a common passion for the Lord's work, and communicate that passion to God's household?

Too often we rush to decisions, relying on our personal perspective and experience, rather than on the guidance of the Holy Spirit.

The answer remains today what it has been since the beginning, namely, time spent together in the basic discipline of prayer. Too often we rush to decisions, relying on our personal perspective and experience, rather than on the guidance of the Holy Spirit. This is not to say that God will not use our abilities and insight in the service of the church. However, self-reliance is a persistent problem that must be countered with the attitude of humility and communication with the Head of the church.

Many times, the private and council prayer of elders is focused on the needs of people in the flock, or the concerns of specific ministries, and these are important. Nevertheless, the sine qua non frequently lacking is intensive *prayer for wisdom* in making decisions for the people of God. Unless we preface our discussions and debates on policy with corporate prayer for the Holy Spirit's direction of our thinking, our individualism will dominate our proceedings and efforts. Are we being honest about whether our prayers precede our decisions, or, in fact, do our petitions implore the Lord to shore up our previously laid plans, even overcome the defects in our already concluded resolutions?

Furthermore, if the council is to find the mind of Christ on issues, our praying must be more than the perfunctory, "Lord, give us wisdom tonight." We need to be willing to talk to the Lord in front of our brothers about the same specific concerns and disagreements that we know will be surfaced in the debate to follow. If we are having difficulty reaching a considered consensus, does not that mean we should ask the Lord to give us a breakthrough, even change minds? The investment of time in prayer in fact will smooth and hasten our progress.

THE ROLE OF THE PREACHER

The next obstacle to governance by consensus to be tackled forthrightly is the role played by the church's primary or most prominent preacher. If the pulpit is filled by one man, true of many evangelical churches, the extent of his exposure to the congregation is disproportionate to the amount of contact the other elders have with the people. His influence over the flock can tempt him to either take on or accept a superior or (even worse) dictatorial role. Preservation of the principle of the equality of the elders is often challenged severely by the role played by the elder who is the primary preacher, the "senior pastor."

In *The Walk-On-Water Syndrome,* Edward B. Bratcher analyzes pastoral and church failures, and the factors that make the personal defeats of pastors inevitable. A rampant problem is the unbiblical elevation of the preacher: an unconscious, but sometimes deliberate, seductive conspiracy between the preacher, the congregation, and the ruling body of the church, each of whom have a vested interest in setting the man up on a pedestal. If the preacher is popular and able, the congregation is willing to idealize, elevate, and honor him. The preacher believes, or is persuaded by such adulation, that his effectiveness is improved by his enhanced position. And finally, the acquiescent ruling body believes that having a celebrity is an important factor in the church's success and growth.[71] No wonder the man is tempted to become a dictator. But we—the congregants or the leaders—are not guilt-free. Are we not, like Israel of old, asking for a king like the other nations have, a convenient and comfortable arrangement we believe will solve our problems?

Such a regrettable collusion need not be the case, and many exemplary exceptions could be cited. Nothing is inherently counterproductive or wrong with having a lead preacher if he is humble—and truly and publicly honors the efforts and gifting of the other elders. He will take pains to teach the congregation that he is only one member of a team that shares in the work of the church. He will make clear his conviction that his role is based on his God-given gifting, not on power, or worse, by virtue of his ordination. Among others, John Piper, at Bethlehem Baptist Church in Minneapolis, is an excellent example of a preacher who has retained the title of senior pastor without elevating himself above the other elders of the church. Piper is highly committed to his equality with the other elders and he reflects this attitude in his writing on this point.

Biblical leadership is best promoted by dropping the title "pastor" and using the biblical term "elder" in its place. If the elder who does the preaching takes on the title of "pastor," while the other elders are referred to as "elders," the task of sustaining the perception of elder equivalence before the people will be almost impossible. Both Peter (1 Peter 5:1) and John (2 John 1, 3 John 1) refer to themselves as elders even though they were recognized as apostles. These servants considered both their equality with other church leaders and the true nature of their responsibilities to be more important, and in need of being more frequently stressed, than any assertion of the authority of their apostolic position.

A pastor who will not submit to a peer relationship with other pastors of the church also will not submit to a peer relationship with its other elders.

Routinely, the single preacher of a small church "steps up" into the position of senior pastor as more staff members are added to serve the growing congregation. Yet, in such circumstances, when several men on staff are equally capable of conducting the full range of pastoral duties, the risk to elder equivalence is accentuated. If the first man assumes the supposedly prerogative-, or honor-laden, part of senior pastor, he makes it clear that he is not willing to accept peer accountability or to consider other staff as having equal worth. Moreover, the senior pastor will find it difficult to serve as an equal of the other elders if he already considers himself superior to all the staff. To put it another way, a pastor who will not submit to a peer relationship with other pastors of the church also will not submit to a peer relationship with its other elders.

Delving deeper into this widespread problem, we find that it is not really the title of senior pastor or his leadership role that is at fault. The dilemma is that the church has long been afflicted with an alien power structure, in which one man leads by virtue of his position, rather than because of his gifting. Commentator Brian Shilhavy traces the roots of the corruption of the role of the pastor to the Reformation:

> Much of American evangelical Christianity has its roots in the reformation movements of Europe. The reformers of Europe (Luther, Calvin, Zwingli, etc.) broke ranks with the

established churches of their day, particularly the Roman Catholic Church and the Church of England. They did much to reform theology (salvation by faith in Christ alone), and to make the Bible available to the masses with translations into the vernacular of the people. Many, such as William Tyndale, the father of the English translation of the Bible, gave up their life [sic] in their fight against the established church of their day. However, as new churches and denominations were formed, they retained the concept of centralized authority within the church, and there was actually very little "reforming" of church leadership structures. Thus, in many denominations, the *priest* was simply replaced in most churches with a *pastor* (i.e., Lutherans, Presbyterians, etc.), although there were some exceptions, like the Plymouth Brethren, who believed in a plurality of elders rather than a centralized leader-pastor. The Anabaptist denominations, which came over to America largely from Britain, also retained this centrality of leadership.[72]

The congregation and the elders need leadership. However, it is unlikely (and unbiblical to claim) that the Lord has granted all the leadership gifts for all aspects of ministry, or the "most important" abilities, to one individual. No matter that this is often asserted.

Randy Pope, senior pastor of the large Perimeter Church in suburban Atlanta, relates the difficult process of successfully achieving consensus on the church's ministry plan with his elders. From church consultant Lyle Schaller he received the following advice, which he recommends in his book, *The Prevailing Church*. Schaller "described the ideal process":

I, as the pastor, should have, in his words, "gone to the mountain to seek the voice of God." After believing I had heard His voice, I should then go back to our elders, who in our system of polity function as my authority. He recommended that if the elders could not, at that point, affirm my sense of God's leading, then I should go once again to the mountain, spending time listening to God. Whether I sensed that God would lead in the same way I had perceived on my first trip, or whether I sensed that God would lead in a different direction, I should share that with our elders. If, again, they could not embrace this new vision, then perhaps yet another such mountain visit and subsequent reporting should take place. If, however, after three times we could not agree, Lyle suggested that I should then resign. If the elder team and I could not agree on vision, then I, as the subordinate in our polity, should seek another opportunity of service where my vision and my leadership direction could be in harmony.[73]

In sharp contrast, in a discussion of pastoral leadership and church-governing structure, Doug Goins, one of the team of elders who shares the pulpit at the North Peninsula Bible Church in Palo Alto, California, was asked who was in charge: "Tell me what aspect of our ministry we are discussing, and then I will tell you who is in charge. It is different for outreach, member development, church planting, and so forth."[74]

**Pastors who accept other pastors as equals
are much more likely to welcome other elders
onto the team as equal participants.**

For some, like the Peninsula Bible Churches (North and South), an alternative to the senior pastor-led church is the New Testament practice of team ministry. It offers several advantages. The pastors, especially those who preach, demonstrate teamwork, including its necessary components: differentiation of labor according to gifting, honoring each other's gifts, and, most important, humility. Pastors who accept other pastors as equals are much more likely to welcome other elders onto the team as equal participants. The effect of this practice—of team ministry—on the growing church that is adding preaching staff is this: now that others have been added to the team, that talented founding pastor is released to spend significant time with other congregants, including potential leaders in ministries of the church, and to apply the instruction of Ephesians 4:11–12: "He [Christ] gave some as . . . pastors and teachers, *for the equipping of the saints for the work of service, to the building up of the body of Christ*" (italics added).

On this point, George Barna's wide exposure to churches around the world has led him to conclude that the church has only a few extraordinary solo leaders:

But most people do not have the mix of gifts, talents, experience, and opportunity that has enabled these individuals to gain notoriety. The fact that few people possess such incredible leadership capacity is an important realization, for it means that most churches are resigned to one of two outcomes: consistent failure due to lack of available high-impact leaders or reliance upon a different leadership paradigm.[75]

This turning to another paradigm is precisely what I am advocating: establishing team ministry for leadership of the church.

DOMINATION BY ONE OR A FEW

The senior pastor model is not the only peril stalking our ruling by consensus. Other pervasive, systemic plagues arise from the procedures church organizations use to function. Often these methods prevail over the church's institutional statements (stated polity), the old "what-we-do-doesn't-match-what-we-say" phenomenon. Two such threats stand out: control of the elder council by one, or by a few. Either the council is dominated by one man, or the real decision-making for the church is conducted by a small select group, or by the paid staff, with minimal council involvement.

The customary and prudent practice is for an elder council to have a moderator to chair orderly meetings, assure fairness, and promote the decision-making process. More the better if he is also able to keep the men focused on the agenda issues and end meetings on time! However, the position of moderator must never be transformed into some type of superior head of the elder council. Nor is the post to be used to impose the will of any one elder on the council.

Often the senior pastor or a strong entrenched leader occupies the post of chairman. A senior pastor, or the lead pastor on a staff of multiple pastors, is usually an able man with a passion for various ministries of the church. He very well may be the ideal advocate of ministry proposals, but his taking the role of the chairman of the council is counterproductive for him and his compatriots. The work of the godly effective moderator is to see that issues are addressed and determinations made in a biblical manner, after prayer and discussion in which all participants were both heard and understood. He presides to mediate, restrain, clarify, and expedite: he is not singled out to direct the body of elders down a predetermined path or one of his own choosing. He is not put in charge to control, but to serve the group. If the man considers the position of the chair as entailing prestigious stature or rights, or if the others acquiesce in such an arrangement, this amounts to the denial of the equality of the elders.

Advice against having a prominent church leader in the position of moderator is consistent with the findings of those who have studied interactions in industrial groups in which a manager tries to moderate the discussion.[76] At one and the same time, he is the person most passionate about a new idea (his), *and* in charge of encouraging debate and critique, while required to remain neutral and silent! This conflict in his roles precludes the manager's effective facilitation in such deliberations. Far better to delegate the responsibility-intensive job of moderator to a man known for his wisdom, fairness, equanimity, and humility, and to set the standard that he facilitate, not direct.

Another menace to be avoided is domination of the elder council by a few, a danger that may flow from the polity of the church: in practice, the paid staff or a small number of leaders really run the church, with little elder council participation. Such governance of the church by the professionals is a transgression of the biblical mandate for elder leadership. Further, this will result in a dearth of indigenous leadership, the inevitable outcome because motivating men to take on responsibility when they have no accompanying sense of ownership is difficult to impossible.

Leadership by a single man or an oligarchy (a small circle of handpicked leaders) is a direct violation of the biblical standard of a true plurality of elders. For collegiate decision-making to succeed, a sufficient number of men must examine each proposal through the filter of independent thinking to achieve consensus. Acceptance of the domination of the elder council by one or a few is a serious lapse in responsibility by the elders.

FUNCTIONAL BARRIERS TO LEADING BY CONSENSUS

Besides the hazards previously discussed, there are several functional barriers relating to elder councils—and efforts at shared leadership in general—which are also significant impediments to achieving decisions by consensus. These are micromanagement, inadequate preparation, inappropriate use of *Robert's Rules of Order*, bias, and short-term memory. In this section, the ill effects of these influences will be delineated. The remedies will be explained later, under Handling the Major Decisions (p. 142).

MICROMANAGEMENT

The frequently voiced complaint—"We have too many meetings and they are boring and too long"—correlates with the principle, emphasized by business authors Robert Nelson and Peter Economy, that productive meetings should involve only "those people who have a commitment to the topic to be discussed."[77] The problem can be alleviated by bringing to the council meeting—placing on the council's agenda—only those matters requiring the consideration of the whole council and limiting discussion to agenda items only. To achieve this, an efficient council will delegate much of its work to subgroups.

Meetings should involve only "those people who have a commitment to the topic to be discussed."
Robert Nelson and Peter Economy

Even when councils do delegate, they still often unnecessarily reexamine matters, frustrating the assigned subgroup by making its efforts seem irrelevant. This is micromanagement; the whole council has resorted to rehashing a matter that was best handled by a few, and has in essence rescinded its previous delegation.

INADEQUATE PREPARATION

If an advocate of an initiative is seeking a ruling by an elder council that has not been sufficiently prepared, the entire deliberative process (and quite possibly the result) will be inadequate, obstructed, and discouraging. (The proper role of the advocate is discussed below.) And, as has been said before, when the council chooses to create policy by means of the debate of the entire group, it is operating unproductively, as a committee of the whole. The same thing happens when a submitted proposal cannot be handled with a simple up or down decision, and the council is forced to develop modifications then and there. These procedures are inefficient and unsatisfactory, and the participants leave the experience frustrated. Facets of inadequate preparation include:

- The council has not previously built a biblical framework for interpreting new issues.

- Members of the elder council lack personal or sufficient knowledge of the subject at hand.

- Supporting details and arguments are not made available with the proposal beforehand.

137

- Insufficient time has been allowed for members to study the issue before they face the obligation to decide.

INAPPROPRIATE USE OF *ROBERT'S RULES OF ORDER*

In their bylaws, many churches refer to *Robert's Rules of Order* for the standard procedures to be used in their official meetings. *Robert's Rules* are based on a parliamentary model for deliberative assemblies, and designed to make clear the rights of both the majority and the minority, and to deal with situations in which there may be impassioned division of opinion.[78] Therefore, *Robert's Rules* are intended for the very division prohibited in Scripture, a multiple party system. Tragically, this model does not aid decision-making by consensus or promote unity. *Robert's Rules* literally fosters the majority's imposition of its will on the minority.

At the conclusion of contentious council debates conducted under *Robert's Rules*, some men will leave believing they have "won," and some will leave feeling they have "lost." The latter will not find it easy to support the outcome of the voting.

Robert's Rules are intended for the very division prohibited in Scripture, a multiple party system.

Rule 3 requires that, before a proposal may be considered, it must be put before the council as a motion. *Then* it may be discussed, by persons either in support or in opposition. After adequate deliberation, the motion is either approved or disapproved. Unless total council agreement on a proposition is achieved, this procedure produces winners and losers. This is not how consensus is built. The only mechanism in *Robert's Rules* for building consensus is the tedious process of repeatedly amending a proposal until the amended motion receives a near unanimous passage. As Doyle and Straus point out: "This is why, in most formal organizations, including Congress, collaborative problem solving and support building is done informally in caucus before formal meetings."[79]

Another serious problem directly follows from the fact that, usually, the moderator of the elder council is elected to that position because he is a respected and knowledgeable man. Yet, by *Robert's Rules*, in the debate on any motion, the moderator *cannot* state his opinion, so the council is deprived of his wise counsel.

BIAS

Strongly held personal positions impede leadership by consensus. Experienced elders enter any discussion with many previously formed opinions. Frequently, when proffering his group's results to the council, the presenter of a proposal fails to identify immediately the underlying biblical and philosophical considerations involved. As a result, before he secures the listeners' commitment to the base on which he intends to build the argument, the advocate has triggered debate, albeit unspoken debate. As he then tries to build the rationale for the proposal, he finds that he has lost the attention of some elders. Silently, they are busily formulating objections and rebuttals.

Unavoidably, elders' previous involvements, independence, personal positions, and prejudices—some rigid—obstruct their objective consideration of new proposals. If, at the outset, the firm Scriptural principles supporting the subject at hand had been established, the men's natural tendencies to object would have been curbed. The elders would have been enabled to set aside bias. Men are often unaware of personal predispositions: we must assume we have them and work on correction and containment.

SHORT-TERM MEMORY

The last functional impediment to consensus leadership to be mentioned here is simply our inability to remember. Since most difficult matters are not clearly black or white, propositions must be considered and decided based on the *preponderance* of the positives against the negatives. Those offering an initiative frequently do not set the stage for an expeditious productive assessment of the issues. They neglect the simple device of providing a format by which the council can keep in mind all the pro and con elements. Participants in a discussion will find it difficult to concentrate on multiple arguments at one time. As we listen to the points that follow, we do not retain the previous arguments. In other circumstances, this is an asset, how we are designed. For instance, this filtering ability of the mind allows us to listen to a single conversation in the midst of many others in a crowded restaurant.

However, in a meeting, men will focus on either what the last speaker just said, on what the current participant is saying, on unrelated thoughts triggered by a contributor, or on planned rebuttals to a previous point. As a result, unless a mechanism is provided to assist the participants' short-term memory, the discussion and voting tend to be reactive to the last statements made and not to the total weight of the evidence. The frustration the presenter experiences (shared by all present), is partially a manifestation of the limitations of short-term memory, aggravated by a presentation technique that did not take this into consideration.

THE ROLE OF THE MODERATOR

Profitable deliberations, productive meetings, and decisions by consensus do not proceed out of our innate abilities, but out of intentional godliness and discipline. Of all the elders deliberating a matter, the council's moderator bears the greatest burden. Scripture is specific about the godly character of the elder, but several traits are vitally important in a moderator:

- **1 Timothy 3:2–3**: temperate, prudent, not pugnacious, gentle

- **Titus 1:7–8**: not self-willed, not quick-tempered, not pugnacious, just, self-controlled

Godly leadership is demonstrated through these attributes and *not* through the exercise of power. Building unity in the council, and enhancing its ability to arrive at decisions each elder is willing to own personally, depends on the character of the moderator and his skill in achieving consensus.

The title *moderator* is preferable to that of chairman.

The obligations of the delegated point man, the moderator of the council of elders, are not insignificant. Through wise, godly team management, he is charged with making sure the governing body is responsive to the needs of the congregation and that all activities of the church are given effective leadership. He will achieve this, not by personally directing ministries or other elders to take certain leadership duties, but by laying each need or situation before the council, and guiding its work so that one (or more) of his elder equals takes up each area that needs direction and shepherding. The job of the moderator also entails working through an efficient feedback and accountability structure to track (for the council) whether each elder is carrying out his delegated responsibilities. Because of these duties and the need to prevent the power relationship connotation, the title *moderator* is preferable to that of chairman.

In the council meeting, the moderator's duty is to regulate the discussion, to assure that all participants are heard and treated respectfully in the process, and to see that the meeting's agenda is followed and covered. The moderator is the chief enforcer of the biblical imperatives for personal conduct as applied to the dynamics of the council meeting. In the ideal council, where plurality is esteemed, *all* the elders have equal authority, but *each* possesses different gifts, background, experience base, and ministry callings. This allows each man to bring a unique contribution to the council. But neither he nor his fellows are allowed to display these—the Spirit's gifts to the church—if the moderator fails, or is erratic, in his supervision. Each man needs to know his own gifting and the moderator should be intentional in recognizing the differing gifting of council members.

These imperatives for the moderator are certainly clearly understood in the secular world. Note these words of wisdom from John Carver, a leading expert on the proper behavior of corporate boards and author of *The CarverGuide* series on effective board governance:

> As the chairperson of the board, your role, on behalf of the board, is to protect and further the integrity of governance. . . .Your role of chairperson comes as close to a pure instance of Robert Greenleaf's servant-leader as I can imagine. You are clearly the board's leader and just as surely its servant as well. Your job is not to lead the organization—it is the far more sensitive and demanding task of helping the board to lead the organization.
>
> It is your responsibility to understand servant-leadership, understand governance process, and understand how a group of peers—all of whom bring diverse values—can be visionary, bold, and pragmatic all at the same time. Your job is as much about nurturance as about cracking the whip, as much about thorough deliberations as about decisiveness, and as much about stimulating diversity as about reaching a single official decision. Your job is to encourage, cajole, pressure, and cheerlead your board to be all it can be.[80]

HANDLING THE MAJOR DECISIONS

Many decisions the elder council must make are straightforward and encounter uncomplicated, expeditious approval. Especially this is true when proper delegation has been followed and problems have been previously ironed out by those gifted to address each type.

However, some issues require deliberation by the whole council. Examples are doctrinal positions, revision of bylaws, senior staff changes, property purchases, building programs, church-planting proposals, and major new initiatives. Such judgments warrant extra effort from the council and its moderator to assure thoughtful, thorough consideration, and the council's full ownership of, and support for, the resulting resolutions.

**The man most committed to the matter's success
should be entrusted and empowered
to be the proposal's advocate.**

All of us must avoid bringing complex and controversial issues *directly* to the full council. Such subjects, especially those that are controversial, are much more successfully addressed if initially considered by a small designated group of elders. To these is delegated the task of researching the issue, studying the biblical implications, and preparing material for the members to review prior to the council's discussion. This group may also be charged with drafting a proposal to be presented by one of their number, the advocate, to the entire council for debate. This procedure not only better equips the council for God's work, but assures the efficient use of the least possible amount of council meeting time.

THE ADVOCATE

In a vigorous body, initiatives for change in the church should emanate from any church member, elder, or staff person, as the occasion demands, as well as from the efforts of the long-term planning team. Because the elders are those biblically charged with the direction of the church, it is best (and a sign of good health) when proposals are initiated by council members, instead of being introduced by staff. (Of course it is always appropriate for the council to ask staff to research and develop a proposal that will be presented to the council for its review.)

COUNCIL DECISIONS

Because the elder council is comprised of equals with many gifts, no one man has the permanent role of being the source of new ideas. The man most committed to the matter's success and, it is hoped, the most gifted in the area pertaining to the initiative under consideration, should be entrusted and empowered to be the proposal's advocate.

INTRODUCING THE TOPIC

The advocatory process of a proposal ought to incorporate a number of elements. Once he is delegated the task, or desires to bring forward an initiative on his own, the council member advocate should notify the council that he is formulating an initiative for presentation at a particular time (subject to the moderator's scheduling). Only the scope of the proposal is necessary at this stage. For instance, the advocate might say: "The Lord is impressing on me that we have reached the point at which we should consider planting a church, and I am willing to spearhead a proposal." Once the council gives its approval, the advocate asks the other elders to pray, to ask God to confirm His leading and give wisdom for examination of all aspects of the project. Also, he should invite other members to contribute their suggestions for assembling the initiative. The addition of another elder or two to assist in preparing the proposal is the council's prerogative. So is its decision about when the congregation will be included in the forthcoming discussion and given the chance to furnish their ideas and opinions.

PREPARING THE PROPOSAL

Next, the advocate gathers a small set of the most committed and knowledgeable proponents; they may be elders, staff, or members. Opportunity must be provided for anyone interested in the matter— staff, elder, or congregant—to offer their input. The advocate, or a member of his team, should locate and meet with those in the church who will be most directly affected, to discuss the working proposal and solicit their suggestions. The more significant the effect will be on a person's area of involvement, the more critical his early inclusion in the proposal's preparation.

Some opposition always occurs when any change is proposed and should not necessarily dissuade an initiator from proceeding. In fact, objections surfaced at this stage are very valuable and should not be brushed aside. Careful attention to points raised by those with reservations assist the advocate in making adjustments which will preclude the difficulties or strengthen his rationale for the proposal.

The more significant the effect will be on a person's area of involvement, the more critical his early inclusion in the proposal's preparation.

Next, the advocate and his team prepare a draft report and set of briefing charts which describe the initiative in detail and will be used when the presentation is made to the council. The charts should address:

- The need that prompts the initiative

- The proposed solution and resources required

- The benefits and disadvantages of the proposed solution

- The alternatives that were considered

- The consequences of not acting on the proposal

Email exchange of drafts by those in the advocacy group is an efficient technique for working through several revisions and avoiding time-consuming meetings as the refining process proceeds. A wide range of opinions helps the group in improving its proposal and should surface any possible negative consequences. The latter must be added to the charts, and, where possible, dealt with through modifications in the proposal which will eliminate conflicting outcomes. Better to bring potential problems out into the open, alongside the preponderance of positive results. Any alteration of the status quo will have some repercussions. If the potential complications are ignored, the council will believe it is being "sold a bill of goods."

The advocate's rehearsal of the presentation in front of his team, before he offers it to the elder council, will catch omissions and correct any lack of clarity.

PREPARING THE COUNCIL

Copies of the proposed initiative, supporting materials, and the actual motion to be offered after debate is concluded, should be distributed to the elders a reasonable amount of time before the council meeting, so the men may study the proposal and put questions to the advocate in advance. The advocate will be more successful in cultivating consensus if he can capture any negative sentiment prior to the meeting, and either modify the proposal to alleviate the concern, or add arguments that put the opposing considerations in perspective.

Understandably, an elder may be upset when a recommendation that will have a significant effect on his specific sphere of concern in the church is introduced without his prior consultation. We need the frequent reminder that *love is imperative* in an elder council! Love entails the obligation that, before the council meeting, a member of the advocacy team will meet with any brother who will be affected by an impending initiative. It is especially important not to blind-side a man in the actual deliberative session. Any man with a known bias may be ministered to in the same way. Time spent personally answering his questions ahead of time will reassure him, and will spare the council contentious proceedings.

The moderator must demonstrate his leadership in adequately preparing the council to be *ready* to make a decision: He should impress the men with both the context and the degree of urgency entailed.

PRESENTATION TO THE COUNCIL

The presentation to the council should be made by an able presenter. This may be the advocate, a member of his team, or another person the council trusts. And, the principle of good preparation operates in the conduct of the presentation as well. This is especially true when laying the biblical foundation and navigating emotionally charged waters.

The key element is that the presenter must *first* gain the council's agreement on the biblical principles that will govern the decision *before* the main issue is presented. Disorganized thoughts and aroused emotions will impair the men's ability to evaluate a proposal's spiritual imperatives. If initially bypassed, the discussion of the fundamental biblical issues involved will become hopelessly entangled in the debate later with the merits of the proposal and the pragmatic considerations.

In addition, if the advocate's introduction is handled in a temperate, prudent, respectful, and gentle manner (1 Tim. 3:2–3), initial reactions are mollified and passions drained, so that the component parts of the initiative can be considered with clear minds. For example, if the council is weighing the wisdom of a taking out a mortgage, versus waiting for up-front contributions before proceeding with a facility expansion, it is important that the council review first its previous decisions regarding borrowing. On sensitive matters, adequate time must be allowed for the Holy Spirit to develop understanding and ownership. This gives each man time to put aside his own bias, and for his confidence in the final position taken by the council to take shape.

For the actual council deliberations, the presenter should be prepared with paper handouts, a whiteboard, flip chart, computer presentation, or alternative. The pros and cons should be evaluated as well as the key reasons supporting approval of the proposal, and the drawbacks and impediments stated in parallel columns. As the discussion continues, he (or the facilitator; see below) should add the council's suggestions to the chart. By the time the council attempts to reach a consensus, the men will be looking at a summary of the points made by the presenter and contributed by the elders, effectively overcoming the participants' short-term memory limitations.

The presenter's skill and fairness in capturing the essence of elders' contributions are critical in achieving a final consensus.

The presenter's skill and fairness in capturing the essence of elders' contributions are critical in achieving a final consensus. He may not ignore or minimize any expressed reservations. However, under the guidance of the moderator, the council retains the responsibility to debate the relative significance of these.

The decision process is advanced if the elders are reminded that, in almost every case, they are not making a decision for or against something. In fact, they are choosing one of several alternatives. One option is inaction. Another, delay. However, these also have consequences, which are best objectively quantified during the debate.

FACILITATOR OR MODERATOR?
Obviously, effective leadership is essential for the church. Someone must first see to it that all ministries are provided the efficacious

guidance so essential to the church, and next that the decisions of the council are carried out. Someone will have to handle matters between council meetings, that is only those matters that fall within the framework of just those aforementioned decisions. To cover this requirement, usually a strong, capable man is chosen to be the council moderator and is given a title implying power, such as chairman. Immediately the elder is being asked to wear two incompatible hats, that of the impartial facilitator of council debate, and that of an effective leader for the church.

The imperative need of impartiality for the moderator is set in sharp relief by insights from various authorities on the conduct of meetings. First, *Robert's Rules of Order,* Rule Against Chair's Participation in Debate:

> The impartiality required of the chair in an assembly precludes his exercising these rights [to debate] while he is presiding. . . . To participate in debate, he must relinquish the chair; . . . [and] should not return to it until the pending main question has been disposed of, since he has shown himself to be a partisan as far as that particular matter is concerned.[81]

Second, those who study group dynamics recognize the inherent conflict involved when a manager tries to facilitate an effective meeting. Doyle and Straus explain:

> Some bosses may find this difficult to live with at first, but it is almost impossible to run a fair, nonmanipulative meeting when you have a personal investment in the subject matter. There is no way you can objectively lead a group that is considering whether or not to discontinue a project of your own. Even if you try not to influence the group, you will find that your body language reinforces those who want to keep your project going. Your eyes will light up when someone says something reinforcing. You will shrug or frown when you disagree—or more likely, openly object. It is only human. You should be in the group fighting for your ideas, not trying to lead the group toward a rational decision.[82]

What can be done about this inherent conflict in the position of the council moderator, expected at one and the same time to be impartial *and* to provide firm leadership? There are three ways to deal with this problem. The first is the usual: The moderator or chairman conducts himself as a partisan in the discussion, essentially acting improperly by exercising an unfair advantage over the other elders, and, in fact, suppressing the achievement of a true consensus. A second is the classic approach of having whoever chairs the council meeting remain totally neutral, as *Robert's Rules* dictates. The trouble with this practice is that the council is thereby denied the wisdom and influence of one of its most gifted members.

A third method is preferable: The moderator or chairman *appoints* a skilled facilitator from the council, a man who is willing to be neutral on the issue at hand, who will advance the discussion just to the point at which the chair senses that consensus has been achieved and the decision can be formalized by a motion for a vote. In this approach, the moderator may take an active part in the debate and be helpful to the council as it examines the question.

We should honor those men on our councils who are gifted facilitators and stalwart in the character traits mentioned above. Facilitating consensus is such a valuable asset to the council that men should be trained in this skill. It will be apparent that certain elders are better at this work than others, and they should make the effort or be assigned to mentor those who need to develop the ability to facilitate consensus.

THE *ROBERT'S RULES* DILEMMA

Reaching consensus also requires working around the counterproductive *Robert's Rules*. If adherence to *Robert's Rules* is required by the church's bylaws, and an exception is not allowed, the following procedure is worthwhile. As soon as a motion is put before the council, it is bound by *Robert's Rules*, and the council is locked into a potentially divisive procedure. Therefore, instead, the moderator encourages the council to work toward a consensus informally *before* he allows the final, agreed-to proposal to be offered as a motion. Then, at that point, *Robert's Rules* will take effect and govern the discussion and voting procedure. *Robert's Rules* are fine for formally ratifying a decision, but they are counterproductive for assisting in encouraging consensus. (If someone objects to this procedure, a vote may be taken to set aside *Robert's Rules* temporarily.)

FACILITATING CONSENSUS

All these considerations lead to several recommendations for advancing consensus. From my observations, for a productive process to unfold, these guidelines are best enforced by the facilitator, with the support of the moderator, and followed by all those present. This is especially important if, initially, there are polarized viewpoints.

- Obtain the consent of all participants to agree to biblical, objective, fair ground rules before attempting resolution of an issue. The facilitator could begin by asking, "How does Scripture say we are to decide such an issue?" "What are the biblical principles we agree on which we can apply to this issue?"

- Assist the men in exhibiting mutual caring and understanding. When deeply held convictions are involved, it is appropriate for a participant to speak with emotion. However, loud exclaiming, or two speaking at once, verbally overriding, or interrupting each other—all are prohibited as ungodly and unprofitable. See that each contributor is heard without interruption before the next speaks. Support participants in clarifying their thoughts: "Help us to understand your concern. Are you saying that . . . ?" "It would help us address your objection if you could break it down, so we can consider the pieces separately."

- Require all participants to attack the *problem* rather than each other. Put the problem on a wall chart, with everyone in a semicircle facing that wall. As ideas are expressed, capture these on other charts on that same wall so that all present can keep the total picture in perspective. The facilitator must protect the meek and chastise anyone who attacks, demeans, or otherwise does not reflect the godly character defined in Timothy and Titus.

- If individual elders take firm stands, try to expose the underlying interests and concerns that brought them to their positions. Such is the advice of the preeminent negotiators Roger Fisher and William Ury, authors of *Getting to Yes: Negotiating Agreement Without Giving In.*[83] Energy spent in the defense of viewpoints is counterproductive and usually leads to adversarial attitudes. An effective facilitator will draw out the parties, and so surface those basic desires and fears that have led to their positions. Since the council elders are committed to the same basic beliefs and biblical principles, their interests are comparable, despite the fact that various men may prefer different approaches of their own design. The facilitator should lead the group in finding new alternatives that will unite the men in addressing the problem before them in a way that is consistent with their core values.

- Help the group brainstorm additional ideas that have the potential of satisfying all interests by expanding the options for mutual gain.[84] As brainstorming proceeds, guide the group in deleting the least useful suggestions from the chart and ranking those remaining.

- The goal is not to have winners and losers after a debate, but that, in addition to developing a workable approach, all come away from the effort with a sense of accomplishment. In the process, a good facilitator has demonstrated to the men the methods for achieving consensus, which is an investment in the council's future endeavors.

HANDLING AN IMPASSE

Whenever a specific proposal is debated, the council may decide to reject or support it. Or it may ask that the advocacy team research the question further and bring back an amended version. However, the moderator should see to it that the matter is not simply dropped, since a real need in the church is being evaluated. A definite time for revisiting the subject must be set.

On the other hand, suppose the time allotted on the agenda for discussion of the initiative is expended and consensus has not been achieved. What happens then? If the moderator forces a vote at that point, the council loses the rich benefit of its agreement. Ever after, the measure suffers from lack of the council's full initial support. The "losers" are faced with the strong temptation to grumble and murmur. And the moderator has not succeeded in using his God-given wisdom to guide his brothers in applying their God-given gifts, and has exhibited this failure before the council. Not only are they and he impaired in future debates, but the incident may have planted doubt in each man's mind. Now the council is not sure of God's leading and not confident of His will.

Happily, there are other options for handling the impasse caused by lack of consensus and no further time at this meeting to address the matter. One choice, particularly if the debate must be continued, is for the moderator to secure the council's agreement to defer some of the remaining business on the agenda to the next meeting so that resolution of the issue may proceed. The alternative is to agree to table the issue and set up a special meeting specifically designed for fully achieving consensus on the question at hand.

Such problematic situations or impasses usually arise because the facilitator was inept, or the council was inadequately prepared, or was attempting to act as a committee of the whole (inexcusable except in an emergency; see Emergency Decisions, page 160) in creating policy.

AVOIDING BAD DECISIONS

Following the procedures outlined above guarantees that our elder council will never make a wrong decision, right? And the fact that we have unanimity or consensus is evidence that we have found the mind of Christ, does it not? Sadly, no. Memories (mine and those of others) are stained with unpleasant recollections of times councils were united, but on the wrong course.

Councils become united, but on the wrong course.

Why is this? Well aware of the phenomenon, students of group interaction tell us what may be happening, and we are well advised to pay attention. They attribute such results to the overly homogeneous nature of the group considering an issue. The group simply lacks the essential ingredients for real debate. Doyle and Straus point out:

> Even if you appoint a committee of brilliant people with somewhat different sets of expertise and background, there is still a danger that their desire to support each other and reach a common agreement will override their independent critical thinking and their investigation of several alternatives. Psychologist Irving L. Janis has labeled this tendency of groups to think alike. He calls it "group-think."[85]

COUNCIL DECISIONS

Groupthink can appear in several guises and it can function no matter what the subject is. If a pastor, pastoral team, or elder council carefully picks men for the council who unquestionably support them or their philosophy of ministry, groupthink may operate on all issues. In this case, the principle of plurality of eldership—and the requisite debate between independent men to determine Christ's will for the church—have been obliterated by the choice of philosophical look-alikes.

Proper independence must be understood. It is not assertive refusal to join brothers in consensus. Nor is it individualism. It is the recognition that God's will is brought out by the interaction of the separate (independent) insights of a number of elders, each *differently* gifted, and armed with a unique set of experiences. Therefore, each man must realize that God has placed him in the council with his particular gifts and understandings for a purpose. He must express the thoughts the Holy Spirit gives him in the discussions. The independent reasoning of each man, for the good of the whole, is God's design.

However, after careful debate and exposure to diverse views, even a properly constituted council that makes godly decisions in most areas will fail on a particular issue if the men view themselves or the church as being threatened. Consequently, they will become overly defensive, and adopt what is commonly called a "foxhole mentality."

While agreeing that these perils of human nature can lead to bad decisions, I believe that inadequate spiritual and attitudinal behaviors may be at work. Examples of these are:

- Placing a higher value on loyalty to another individual, or to one's church, than to Christ. Supporting a leader because "he is important to the success of the church," rather than finding the mind of Christ as it bears on all decisions.

- Framing an issue in terms of protecting the institution rather than dealing with the biblical and moral issues involved.

- Protecting the institution rather than the congregation by adopting a we-them mentality. Acting as if the leadership's position is more important than God's people, whom we are charged with protecting.

COUNCIL DECISIONS

- Failing to evaluate the full effect of decisions on individuals, including those not directly in view in a decision.

- Giving priority to practical considerations over biblical principles. Inadequate biblical study and grounding by individual council members or the whole group.

- Perfunctory praying—"Lord give us wisdom tonight"—versus wrestling in prayer over the details of the problem prior to the council debate.

- Suppressing debate: either by failing to explore the thoughts and opinions of a brother who is uncertain of a proposed course, or by allowing the intimidating position of a particularly opinionated man to stand unchallenged.

- Being arrogantly overconfident of the council's wisdom. Therefore, not consulting other churches or exploring how similar issues have been handled by the evangelical church historically.

- Being peacekeepers, rather than peacemakers. Failing to deal properly with affairs out of the fear of disturbing the supposed peace, unity, and prosperity of the church.

- Compromising biblical principles because of apprehension of lawsuits or loss of church income.

An additional condition, which has been previously defined, will invariably lead to imperfect, if not wrong, decisions. A council (of more than seven members) operates as a committee of the whole in designing the solution to a challenge, instead of properly delegating the task to a smaller group. Groups of more than seven men are ill-suited to formulate policy, especially in a constrained time span.

These attitudes and actions are disturbing, and are not just possibilities. If we are honest, we have all joined in one or more. Making decisions for the church is a very serious responsibility and requires hard work and prayer. The task cannot be undertaken lightly. One day we elders will stand before Christ and answer for the choices we have made.

DISSEMINATING THE DECISION

The congregation should not be taken by surprise. If its elder council has laid the foundation well, the people (at least the affected portion) will be expecting an announcement that a decision has been made. Beyond making a determination, the council is responsible for fully explaining its decision to the flock. Any major undertaking should be thoroughly understood by the leadership of all ministry teams, and how it affects each team should be laid out. Every available avenue of communication should be exploited. If the decision involves any doctrinal issues, the biblical teaching is imperative, from the pulpit and in other teaching venues.

The possibility always exists that some people may not understand or be in favor of the decision. Since the elders have selected the solution deemed best for the church, those who have difficulties with the decision should be assured that the council arrived at its conclusions prayerfully, through an extended process that included congregational participation.

INVOLVING THE CONGREGATION

How the elders relate to God's people is of paramount importance. How we hear their concerns, the degree to which we include them in the decision-making process, and how we communicate decisions to them must be reviewed at this point. Elders are accountable for encouraging the church body in the work of ministry and for recognizing the priesthood of all believers: "You are a chosen race, a royal priesthood" (1 Peter 2:9). The elders must be constantly preparing men and women to do the work of ministry, "the equipping of the saints for the work of service, to the building up of the body of Christ" (Eph. 4:12). Moreover, elders must protect the flock from ecclesiastical barriers to service. Leadership must never act as a layer between the individual member and his or her Lord in the work of ministry; members are equipped as they perform the work and as they become involved. But are we following the preferred pattern as we teach, shepherd, and lead?

NEW TESTAMENT PRECEDENT

The New Testament epistles to the churches were all written to deal with specific issues, each affecting a local church. In every case, the apostles address the whole congregation concerned. They explain the difficulty to the entire church, and, most often, urge God's people to do what is right, rather than ordering them to do so.

In no case was a letter written to the church's elders, asking them to meet in closed session to make the decision for the congregation. In each instance, the occasion of the problem was used as an opportunity to teach the full body.

ALTERNATIVES TO CLOSED MEETINGS

Today's common practice of holding *closed* elder meetings cannot be reconciled with the approach the apostles employed when shepherding and teaching the early churches. The most salient consequences of closed meetings are congregational distance from and distrust of the elders, and lack of understanding of the biblical reasoning that enters into their decisions. Therefore, it is imperative that each elder council find a way to make its oversight and decision-making processes transparent and instructive for the people.

Some churches have found it effective to allow *any member* of the congregation who wishes to do so to attend the council's meetings and quietly observe its deliberations. Although only a few members will avail themselves of this opportunity, the invitation itself accomplishes much. Observers will probably tell others about the amount of time spent in prayer for people in council meetings, and the elders' serious diligent efforts on behalf of God's family. What an effective way to teach the application of biblical reasoning and to model mature Christian behavior!

Only those portions of the council meeting reserved for debating, voting, discipline hearings, and review of personnel issues—any sensitive matters that require confidentiality—would be held in a closed session.

However, many elders will be understandably uncomfortable with exposing their unprepared remarks in the actual debate over decisions to such scrutiny, and fear the risk of being misquoted. In addition, the open meeting format will make public the vote of each member of the council. Disunity in the body may be emboldened when it is reported that the council was not unified in its final decision, or when opinions were divided in the debate, even though the final decision was unanimous.

COUNCIL DECISIONS

An alternative that offers most of the advantages of the completely open meeting without the above difficulties is the practice of the council inviting interested congregants to attend the appropriate first part of meetings: elders' prayer, the receiving of reports, elders' interviews of those reporting on ministries, and presentations of proposals for elder action. Only those portions of the meeting reserved for debating, voting, discipline hearings, and review of personnel issues—any sensitive matters that require confidentiality—would be held in a closed session.

The last two exceptions to a policy of having open meetings are obviously valid. Sensitive personnel discussions should be handled in closed sessions to protect the individuals involved. Likewise, holding private disciplinary hearings is logically consistent with the New Testament practice of containing matters of discipline to just those affected: "If your brother sins, go and show him his fault in private; if he listens to you, you have won your brother. But if he does not listen to you, take one or two more with you, so that by the mouth of two or three witnesses every fact may be confirmed" (Matt. 18:15–16; from Deut. 19:15). Therefore, holding closed discussions during the investigation phase of a disciplinary situation, or until the truth is determined fully, is advisable. However, both by example and precept, Scripture says that, when it is a matter of discipline over a major question, the particular rebuke that is to be applied is to be made in public before the gathered church—as an essential component of the discipline process, and as a warning to the congregation (Matt. 18:17).

The decision to reserve as private both the give-and-take debate between elders and the actual voting has very little effect on the congregation's need to be informed, since the proposals, their defense by their advocates, and the final outcomes will be made available later to the members. In Acts 15, those elements are the only ones recorded as having occurred in public. We do not know whether there were additional public or private discussions.

> **The elders must conduct their deliberations in a way that confirms the body's confidence in their leadership.**

Many other procedures contribute to the goal of making the elders' decision-making process more transparent for the church. Regular verbal and written reports to the congregation are essential. These should cover the work and determinations of the elders. Apprising the flock of the concerns the elders will be addressing in the future, and inviting contributions of ideas and specific prayer, help to open up the process. Holding informational forums on a major decision *before* the elders make their final judgment will give members personal access and enhance a good working relationship. The elders must conduct their deliberations in a way that confirms the body's confidence in their leadership, and is consistent with their responsibility to teach the congregation.

The Lord's people should have free entree to their council elders. This will naturally take place if the men of the council are active in ministry, and are, therefore, readily available to the congregation. Also, church members could be encouraged to communicate with the council by means of letters. Any *signed letter* should be copied for all council members and an elder delegated to respond. On the other hand, *unsigned letters* of all kinds should be discarded and ignored. This policy should be well understood by the church.

THE EXAMPLE OF ACTS 15

For clarifying the matter of congregational involvement, a helpful perspective issues from the pattern followed by the New Testament church at the Jerusalem Council, which was called to resolve the question of the circumcision of Gentiles. What is observed here is analogous to an individual church's council deliberations today. This assembly was not, as some allege, a meeting of churches (as some denominations practice). Only the Jerusalem church, its missionaries Paul and Barnabas, the original promoters of circumcision for the gentiles from Jerusalem, and witnesses of the initial disturbance in the church at Antioch were present. No other churches were mentioned. The controversy concerned the conduct in Antioch of men who had come from the Jerusalem church. The process employed by the church was as follows:

- The matter was brought before the elder council (15:4–6).

- The involved parties reported and the question was debated before the apostles and elders (15:4–21). All this took place in front of the congregation (15:12, 22, 25).

- The leaders applied the teaching of Scripture to the subject (15:15–18).

- Consensus among the apostles and elders was achieved, and the church was taught by observing the debate (15:22).

- The congregation respected and obeyed their leadership and concurred with the decision (15:22, 25).

- Action consistent with the decision was taken under the supervision of the elders (15:22–23; 16:4–5).

Since the Lord has provided this model, we ought to strive for the same degree of openness with our flocks. However, the challenge of reserving as confidential some aspects of the elders' work remains.

CONFIDENTIALITY

As discussed above, there will be many occasions when matters must be held in strict confidence. Part of an elder's being above reproach lies in his ability, individually and corporately, to maintain confidentially. But maintaining secrecy on sensitive issues becomes increasingly difficult as the number of individuals involved increases. The dilemma is compounded when there is confusion about what is really private. Councils that consider all that happens at their meetings to be restricted will be dealing frequently with the problem of leaks. Because the church leadership and staff will need to be informed of the council's decisions, described in their context, details of meetings are bound to be unintentionally disclosed. If everything is considered secret, nothing will remain secret.

However, as has been discussed, very little of the council's business should be kept private. If we adopt this approach, that small portion of council business that requires protection can be identified, segregated, and properly guarded. Therefore, the first step in maintaining confidentiality is for the moderator to delineate those areas that, for the protection of individuals or the good of the congregation, must remain restricted. Second, all elders need to understand the time frame for nondisclosure. Ambiguity about the time limits on nondisclosure can destroy the integrity of the confidentiality. For example, the council may decide to keep a decision confidential, but only until the council is able to announce it to all those affected at one time, on a date specified.

**If everything is considered secret,
nothing will remain secret.**

Third, these matters should be recorded in a confidential appendix to the council minutes so the main body of the minutes can be made available to the leadership and staff of the church. I have found it very conducive to unity and ministry effectiveness when staff and leadership are kept as fully informed of the council's planning processes and decisions as possible. Segregation of the minutes is simplified if all confidential matters are dealt with in closed session.

COUNCIL DECISIONS

Failure to adopt this kind of division in the minutes often leads to deliberate omission from the minutes of important facts so as to shield those details, thereby creating confusion about what was decided or the basis for decisions.

It seems evident that the restriction of discussion of those matters designated confidential to only elders within the council must be a covenant the men make with one another as part of their council responsibility. However, exceptions must be made to such a strict policy, and it will be too cumbersome for these exclusions to be approved each time, on a case-by-case basis. Elders may need to consult outside the council with counselors, lawyers, or theologians in order to prepare themselves to address an issue. We must be able to rely on the integrity of each elder to make the proper judgment as to the propriety of consulting with outside experts and as to the likelihood of the person consulted to maintain confidentiality.

Many argue that elders should not discuss any council matters with their wives. Both valid and invalid justifications are made for this conviction. Appropriately, an elder may make the decision that the potential harm to his wife's ability to worship, or to relate to an individual or individuals, is greater than the value to him of her wisdom and prayer for the situation facing the elders. However, I deem it inappropriate and imprudent to deny elders their wives' prayer support and insight. Such a blanket prohibition will be based on the fear that some women cannot maintain confidentiality, or, worse, are gossips. Men with wives that cannot discipline their tongues should not be on the elder council. Such elders are not above reproach.

> **Men with wives that cannot discipline their tongues should not be on the elder council. Such elders are not above reproach.**

The question of whether it is acceptable for elders to share their concerns with their wives must be determined by the particular council. Elders' wives may be given helpful guidelines to school them in their role. For instance, how is a wife to answer those in the congregation who request confidential information of her? A suggested reply might be, "Thank you for expressing your concern, but, in light of my husband's responsibility as elder, I have made a commitment not to discuss such things. Please ask the Lord for wisdom for our elders; they need our prayers." If confidential council information is passed on to her, she must resist the impulse to say, "Oh, yes, I know all about that," and respond, "It sounds like that should be kept confidential. For the sake of all concerned, will you agree with me not to mention it to anyone, so the elders are free to address it? We all need to be careful not to aid any rumors." If an elder's wife hears an alarming report, she could gently ask the informant to speak to an elder—and no one else—immediately. She herself should tell her husband and no other. Elders' wives may always listen lovingly when it is proper to do so, but they must refuse to involve themselves in conversations about matters that are being guarded by the council.

EMERGENCY DECISIONS

Leadership must be armed and ready for the occasional emergency, the imperative of making a decision quickly to safeguard the church or a member. The elder council's proficiency and dexterity in functioning effectively in a crisis are chiefly dependent on how well it has prepared itself beforehand. The preeminent essential is that every elder be adequately versed in biblical teaching: "For the overseer must be . . . . holding fast the faithful word which is in accordance with the teaching, so that he will be able both to exhort in sound doctrine and to refute those who contradict" (Titus 1:7, 9). It is of the utmost importance that council elders are of one mind. This they will be if the men have worked together to understand the implications of scriptural precepts for personal conduct and for the church.

Every elder council should undertake the discipline of working through Alexander Strauch's *Biblical Eldership*, and its companion, *The Study Guide to Biblical Eldership.*[*] This text and workbook have been very successful in helping elder councils think through the implications of Scripture for the governance of the church. To name one benefit: the time spent together discussing their conclusions from Scripture will mature the council, and train the men for dealing biblically and favorably with emergency contingencies. If divided on how to apply biblical criteria, the council attempting to deal with a crisis simply multiplies its difficulties.

The heart-wrenching, but pertinent, example of a destabilizing crisis that all too many churches have faced is the moral failure of an elder or person on the paid staff. Elder councils that have not *worked out biblically in advance* the issues of guarding the flock and the reputation of Christ, judicious discipline, and prudent restoration, often fall apart in such an emotionally charged emergency.

---

[*] *The Mentor's Guide to Biblical Eldership*, by Alexander Strauch and Richard Swartley, is the facilitator's version of *The Study Guide to Biblical Eldership*.

COUNCIL DECISIONS

Several influences intensify the need to have prior agreement on firm disciplinary guidelines, which should be detailed in writing in the church's policies. First, in such a situation, some elders will have a close personal relationship with the fallen individual and may not be able to be objective. Second, one or more elders were probably brought up in homes where children had to cover up and excuse the failings or addictions of parents. Consequently, for these men, this learned, minimizing reaction has become an unconscious, habitual behavior pattern that has followed them into their adult lives. (Even mature Christian men have great trouble extracting themselves from such reaction patterns, and in adopting biblically accurate forms of response.) These elders will have particular difficulty in confronting an ethical failure. Sadly, their reluctance to act ("judge") is sometimes misconstrued or excused as the gift of mercy. And third, those men who have experienced their own moral lapses in the past will be aware of how easy it is to fall into temptation and will be reluctant to discipline another elder.

Together we have looked at the elder council in terms of its overall responsibilities, including making decisions and appointing men to the office of elder. Now it is time to probe the council's governing venue, its periodic meetings. How can these be made more profitable and efficient?

All things must be done properly and in a orderly manner.
1 Corinthians 14:40

Chapter 7

Efficient Council Meetings

ELDERS ARE VERY BUSY PEOPLE, both those who are vocational elders, and those who are managing two careers, eldership and tentmaking. All are sacrificing family and personal time to attend to elders' affairs. However, the church deserves timely direction and leadership so that it may be faithful in handling emerging issues and new opportunities for witness and ministry. Consequently, it is necessary for the moderator and the secretary of the council to plan and conduct its requisite meetings in as efficient manner as possible. The following suggestions are based upon my years of experience and conversations with elders in well-managed churches.

**Attempting to cover everything in the
scheduled meeting practically guarantees
that the work will not be done properly.**

Keeping the council meeting focused is difficult because of numerous priorities on the agenda. In addition to the normal council business, there are the essentials of prayer and worship, fellowship, and discussion of overall issues such as goals and long-term church planning. Attempting to cover everything in the scheduled meeting practically guarantees that the work will not be done properly, and everyone will come away frustrated with the outcome. Therefore, a better procedure is to arrange for regular retreats or off-sites for emphasis on fellowship, special issues, training, or planning. Moving these essential activities off the agendas of regularly scheduled council meetings will ensure that they are shorter, with greater focus and productivity.

A council cannot maintain godly conduct and unity during difficult debates if close personal relationships do not exist between the men. Loving relationships, based upon intimate knowledge of each other's lives, are essential, and their nurture must be given high priority. The larger the council, the greater the time and effort required, and the endeavor will involve extended, relaxed conversational times which cannot occur in large group settings. Regrettably, the events planned to meet these needs often fall short because they are *too* structured. As a result, so we frequently hear, more personal connection was achieved when several elders shared a ride to a retreat than at the gathering itself. Unstructured, purely relational get-togethers and getaways will greatly enhance fellowship. For example, each elder could invite three other elders and their wives to dinner, or a similar pattern of men getting together for lunch could be arranged. Such opportunities to hear each others' hearts will greatly enrich the work of the more structured council meetings.

To ensure productive and rewarding meetings, the following suggestions include techniques to be employed before, in, and following regular deliberations. Often, small changes will streamline the system and give morale a great boost.

COMMUNICATION

The elder council is charged with many responsibilities, and must process details which seem endless. Much valuable time can be wasted with ineffective and waistful procedures for the transmission of reports, messages, and the like.

The Internet has revolutionized how we stay current, with web pages and email increasingly facilitating communication. To be faithful stewards of each other's time, elders need to be able to use these methods of correspondence. Email is a highly efficient and timesaving way to interface quickly. It forestalls our being forced to hold a meeting each time the exchange of information or opinion is required.[*] Elders may trade draft proposals, either sending these to specific elders or transmitting them to the entire council. Agendas, minutes of meetings, schedules, announcements, church calendar

---

[*] Documents of any length, as well as charts and pictorial material, can be attached to email messages. Agreement on a common documentation format, such as Microsoft Office ® or Corel/WordPerfect Office ®, will facilitate exchange.

reminders, and so forth can all be expeditiously conveyed. Both public and confidential information may be posted on the church's website, for reference or downloading, with security assured by restricting certain portions to only those persons with password entry.

Web pages are a cost-effective technique for providing all elders up-to-the-minute information on policies, budgets, and activity scheduling. This is far more effective than the alternative of distributing policy manuals and the inconvenience of constantly changing pages. Rare is the elder who has the spare time and enthusiasm for updating these policy manuals.

As congregations become increasingly familiar users of the internet, web pages also become the medium of choice for the elder council to communicate with the people. Reports of elders' activities and decisions can be posted, and members can pose questions, either directed to the council or entered on a church bulletin board for all to see. This information exchange works just like the procedure Internet users follow in accessing technical support people at computer software and hardware venders. At the present time though, churches should exploit this medium while also continuing parallel distribution through bulletin inserts and newsletters.

THE AGENDA AND SUPPORTING DOCUMENTS

When elders believe that council meetings are important to the life of the church and in fact accomplish their purpose, these meetings are valued and the men view their participation positively. To promote this constructive atmosphere, the moderator must make sure that only those matters that warrant the attention of the full council are on the agenda, and that the elders are prepared beforehand to deal with those particular items at the designated meeting.

Readiness for council meetings is enhanced by distribution (well in advance) of an information packet. Usually the council moderator or secretary prepares an agenda and gathers supporting documents: prayer requests, minutes, reports from ministries, copies of proposals, letters, and the like. Whenever possible, these should be distributed early enough and be sufficiently complete that the elders can study the elements and discuss them with their ministry teams or proposal initiators prior to council meetings. Preparation's most worthwhile benefit is that the elders are thereby alerted to be praying about the concerns scheduled for consideration. The information packets also assist those elders who are unavoidably absent in keeping current. These packages should be distributed at least a week before the meeting by means of pickup at the church from a designated location, secure email, or mail delivery.

Only a true emergency should occasion the introduction at a council meeting of a subject that has not been scheduled in advance, or that is presented without pertinent materials having been previously supplied for review. The ground rule that no nonemergency matter may be introduced at the meeting serves to discipline all involved for organized thinking and preparation. This rule also protects elders from being blind-sided, and permits any elder who must be absent to convey his thoughts on a scheduled topic in writing (by email) or through an elder who will be attending.

Preparing the agenda (with attachments) is quite demanding, but important for three reasons:

- **The agenda prioritizes the items to be considered at the next meeting.** The moderator collects the requests for items to be covered at the next meeting and negotiates who and what will be assigned the available time. He will have to guide the members in honoring the constraint of only bringing those items to the council that require the full body's attention. Matters that can be handled effectively outside the council meeting should be.

  Note that scheduling cannot be handled on a meeting-by-meeting basis. If this is the practice, the urgent will displace the important. Instead, the moderator, in consultation with the council, must set an annual calendar to block out time in coming meetings to prepare for annual budgets, congregational meetings, elder confirmation, ministry reports, elder retreats, planning, and the like.

- **The agenda allocates the time for each subject.** After weighing the items to be discussed, the moderator sets the amount of time each warrants. If this is not done in advance, the meeting will run overtime or scheduled items will not be discussed. The designated periods on the agenda will also help the elders curtail the extent of their remarks, as they observe the time allocated and consider the consequences for others of overrunning their segments.

- **The agenda prepares the council in advance on the issues that will be discussed.** The elders may equip themselves by reading any attached supporting material, asking presenters questions before the meeting, and thinking through and praying about the points.

VIRTUAL MEETINGS

Meetings! Pervasive and invasive! They endlessly swamp our lives. But, though they are a major consumer of our time, the painful truth is most meetings are not the expeditious way of getting the job done. Extra meetings are not the suitable context for research, generation of policies, or planning schedules. And the more people present, the worse the conditions for a positive outcome. A meeting is only necessary:

- When the input of all members at one time is required

- When considerable negotiation is anticipated

- When the council's affirmation or nonapproval of a decision is to be formally recorded

Fewer meetings of shorter duration can be scheduled if much of the council's work is delegated. For example, reports and policy formation are best handled in this way. One or several elders tackle the task, talk to the right experts, secure the best information and resources, and work out the details. The selected leader prepares and submits the draft report by email to the other members of the team for review. Each team member is then able to thoughtfully review the document on his own time, with easy access to his resources, and thereby provide constructive feedback by email. Once the appropriate suggestions of other members, received by returned email, are incorporated, a truly productive, face-to-face meeting finalizes the report for later presentation to the entire council. Or, it may be that the back-and-forth checking has produced a document each team member can sign off on, making a meeting unnecessary.

I have noticed that certain men object to this technique, some because they are unfamiliar with computer applications. But there are others who demand "face-to-face" discussions. They tend to be the men who rely on their physical presence or superior verbal abilities. They may override quieter brothers who do not have this talent, and control the amount of discussion, directing the group toward agreement with their points of view. It is difficult for these men to confine themselves to thoughtful, reasoned written arguments. Also, for the sake of the other brothers, I gently urge those uncomfortable working with computers to learn how to use this valuable resource God has provided.

When men are receptive to this efficient means of communication, the Internet discussion technique works well for large or small groups. Studies have shown that this type of information exchange actually enhances creativity and produces more reasoned results than face-to-face debates. It builds trust and consensus, involves all, uses all gifts, and saves time. We cannot lose sight of the need to make a concentrated effort to free elders for shepherding in person, teaching, family time, and personal study and enrichment.

PRAYER

Praying for God's people, the council's work, and the concerns of the church is a vital part of the elders' role and of their meetings. However, as the size of the congregation and the elder council grows, the time taken in sharing prayer requests also escalates.

Council prayer time is best divided into two segments, one for the needs of individuals in the fellowship, and another for the corporate needs of the congregation, elders' decisions, and the church's mission. Otherwise, the prayer requests of individuals will crowd out prayer for corporate needs.

To reserve a good block of time for prayer and expedite actual praying, requests from church attendees in written form should be collected in advance and made available at the start of the council meeting, or distributed to elders in advance by email or in the meeting's information packet. Whatever the procedure for dissemination of prayer requests, the value of the elders praying together cannot be overestimated. It must be a nonnegotiable agenda item.

In a large church, many prayer requests from individuals may be given (two or so) to each man for follow-up notes or telephone calls. Requests for assistance should be fielded by the church office to the deacons or caring ministry, or handled through another timely, personal method.

MINISTRY REPORTS

Part of the oversight responsibility of the elders is keeping up-to-date on church ministries and administration. Scheduled written and oral reports describing the work of council members and other leaders are necessary for the elders' church-wide oversight. Presenters should be coached on how to give brief concise reports which focus on the information important to the council. Equipping the meeting room for video presentation of computer-generated slides and charts, which can more effectively convey data and conserve time, is now cost-effective. The software for preparing slides greatly simplifies the presenter's task.

MINUTES

Accurate session minutes are important tools for documenting the work of the council. However, the time spent in a subsequent meeting reading minutes and tediously correcting omissions and errors can be eliminated. (However, it is worthwhile to read that portion of the minutes that pertains to any carried-over item.) A very successful method is for the council secretary to email a draft of the minutes promptly after each meeting. All meeting attendees have several days to submit corrections of the draft. The final version of the minutes is distributed in the next elder packet and approved in the following meeting, usually without the need for further discussion.

**When men make sacrifices to attend meetings,
they expect them to be productive.**

The minutes should record attendance, the reports given, the proposals discussed, and the decisions made. In addition, the minutes should list the action items agreed to in the meeting, the names of those who were assigned each task, and expected completion dates. Because most elders are bivocational and subject to many obligations, it is helpful for the secretary of the council to call or email those to whom jobs were delegated midway between meetings to get status updates. When men make sacrifices to attend meetings, they expect them to be productive. At the next meeting, if the scheduled review or decision-making cannot take place because someone did not complete his assigned work, there will be a letdown in morale as well as delay.

Normally minutes only record motions and the final decisions of the council. As a result, the rationale for determinations is lost from the records.[*] However, if major decisions are preceded by the proper

---

[*] See also page 158, Confidentiality.

outside investigation, resulting in position papers and materials used in briefings, the reasoning behind decisions can be captured by handling these documents as attachments to the minutes. Of course, major policies should be gathered in a permanent collection made available to leadership and the congregation, in policy manuals, and on the church's website.

POLICY MANUAL

The minutes of the council meetings capture the approval of, and additions to, council-determined policies for the church. However, the archive of minutes is not a useful place for members and staff to go to locate policies that affect the ongoing life of the church. Therefore, as policies are developed and approved by the council, those that are not limited to a single event should be collected in a user-friendly, indexed form that is easily available and free of any confidential information. For each policy, the date of its approval and the names of those responsible for interpretation and administration should be listed.

Such an accessible policy manual will be especially helpful to new elders and staff as they are added to the team. In addition, it will prevent misunderstandings that could lead to conflict or unauthorized activities. Availability to all concerned of a current version of policies is assured most easily if the policy manual is a document on the church's website.

The maintenance of an effective manual is not a trivial matter:

- The manual must be considered important enough, as a management tool and source of guidance, that sufficient manpower is devoted to its maintenance.

- The manual must be kept current. Otherwise, it will be ignored and the policies of the church inconsistently applied, to everyone's frustration.

- Responsibility for the manual must be clearly established, by delegating its upkeep to an administrator who is likely to remain in the position.

The Challenge

Given the facts, elders are men with a multitude of responsibilities, including the constant need to shepherd the flock (both individually and corporately). And to be as effective as possible, elder meetings must be productive. Throughout the years, I have heard many elders complain that they are hindered in ministry because of the time consumed in meetings. This grieves me. Instead, they should be saying: "That was a great meeting! I rejoice in what the Lord is doing in other elders' ministries. The insights and support I received will help me in my service!"

Guard, through the Holy Spirit who dwells in us,
the treasure which has been entrusted to you.
2 Timothy 1:14

Conclusion

MY PRAYER IS THAT THIS WORK will encourage the adoption of a model of church leadership that is both biblical and productive. For too long we have acquiesced in the belief that the apostolic directives for the leadership and governance of the church were culturally bound to the early church period. Instead, we now know that those instructions were grounded in the apostles' fundamental understanding of the nature of the church and God's intentions for her. These imperatives are immutable. The church is the body of Christ, God's household: it was never intended to be a hierarchical institution in which power was vested in a select few—relegating those men who should be active in leadership as elders to a passive role.

The notion—the poor excuse—that many churches have selected promising, secular leadership structures from the world of commerce merely as expedient methods of accomplishing the mission of the church is overly simplistic. Truth be told, hierarchical, top-down management approaches are driven much more by the engine of men's egos and their desire for control, and far less by the goal of emulating good business practice.

Moreover, the church has a history of being slow to adopt useful management approaches, and even slower to discard those proven to be counterproductive. As early as 1970, in books like *In Search of Excellence*,[86] Tom Peters and Robert Waterman, guided only by empirical observations, exposed the destructive effects of top-down control on creativity and productivity in industry. Why have we church leaders not been equally perceptive? It is not as though we are adrift, without clear biblical direction. Rather, we have been entrusted with the operating manual, God's Word. Shame on us!

We are long overdue in completing the work of the Reformation. In most fellowships, theology has been repaired, but church leadership principles have yet to be conformed to the standards taught

CONCLUSION

in the New Testament. But we must be careful: We should not institute structures that appear to be biblical, but which do not preserve the apostles' spirit and intent, and do not serve our people. Old or new forms that fail either of these tests must be discarded or not attempted in the first place.

The suggestions made in this book must receive the same scrutiny. I believe they express the biblical teachings; they have relevant application in a variety of churches, and are working well in specific churches. This deflates the excuse that the apostles' instructions cannot be applied in our culture. However, I recognize that each congregation represents a different situation, and, where the New Testament is not explicit, differing approaches may be appropriate.

The passages on elder leadership in the church which we have studied together give us more than adequate guidance, if we honestly evaluate their implications, and do not filter our interpretations through our present polities. The key is to demand of each decision, before it becomes policy and practice, these questions: "Does this truly conform to our Lord's intentions for His church?" and "Will it advance His purposes?" The good ends of church growth or evangelism never justify the means if the means harm the family of God.

We cannot take this lightly. As elders, we have an awesome responsibility to Christ, the Head of the church, "to shepherd the church of God which He purchased with His own blood," as those who will be required to "give an account." There will be a test.

May our gracious Lord grant each of us wisdom and courage as we follow His marching orders.

NOTES

1. Alexander Strauch, *Biblical Eldership: An Urgent Call to Restore Biblical Church Leadership*, 3d ed. (Littleton, Co.: Lewis and Roth, 1995).
2. Alexander, *The Study Guide to Biblical Eldership*; and Alexander Strauch and Richard Swartley, *The Mentor's Guide to Biblical Eldership* (Littleton, Co.: Lewis and Roth, 1996).
3. Church consultant and Professor of New Testament Language and Literature, Talbot School of Theology, La Mirada, Calif.
4. 651 North Wayne Avenue, Wayne, PA 19087.
5. Palo Alto, Calif.
6. Larry Osborne, *The Unity Factor: Developing a Healthy Church Leadership Team* (Vista, Calif.: Owl's Nest, 1989).
7. *Leadership Journal,* www.LeadershipJournal.net (20 June 2001).
8. Alexander Strauch, *Ministry of Mercy: The New Testament Deacon* (Littleton, Co.: Lewis and Roth, 1992), 78.
9. David Wallace, "The Semantic Range of the Article-Noun-Kai-Noun Plural Construction in the New Testament," Grace Theological Journal 4 (Spring 1983): 59–84.
10. Ibid.
11. William F. Arndt and F. Wilber Gingrich (translated from Walter Bauer; revised and edited by Frederick W. Danker), *A Greek-English Lexicon of the New Testament and Other Early Christian Literature*, 3d ed. (Chicago: University of Chicago Press, 2000), 861; Gerhard Kittel and Gerhard Friedrich, eds., *Theological Dictionary of the New Testament*, trans. Geoffrey W. Bromiley (Grand Rapids: Eerdmans, 1957), 931–35).
12. Kittel and Friedrich, *Theological Dictionary*, 938–39.
13. Ibid., 818.
14. J. P. Moreland, *Love Your God With All Your Mind: The Role of Reason in the Life of the Soul* (Colorado Springs: NavPress, 1997), 191–92.
15. F. F. Bruce, *The Book of the Acts* (Grand Rapids: Eerdmans, 1988), 231, 282–85.
16. Stephen P. Robbins, *Organizational Behavior*, 8th ed. (Upper Saddle River, N.J.: Prentice Hall, 1997), 347.

NOTES

17. Ibid., 370.
18. Moreland, *Love Your God*, 190–91.
19. Warren Bennis and Patricia Ward Biederman, *Organizing Genius: The Secret of Creative Collaboration* (New York: Addison-Wesley, 1997), 198–99.
20. George Barna, *The Power of Team Leadership* (Colorado Springs: WaterBrook, 2001), 100–106.
21. Ibid., 100.
22. Gorge Barna, *The Habits of Highly Effective Churches* (Ventura, Calif.: Regal, 1999), 52.
23. Strauch, *Biblical Eldership*, 39.
24. Michael Doyle and David Straus, *How to Make Meetings Work* (New York: Jove, 1982), 15.
25. Barna, *Habits of Highly Effective Churches*, 60.
26. Strauch, *Biblical Eldership*, 45–50.
27. Robbins, *Organizational Behavior*, 371.
28. Barna, *Power of Team Leadership,* 71.
29. John Piper and Wayne Grudem, eds, *Recovering Biblical Manhood and Womanhood: A Response to Evangelical Feminism* (Wheaton, Ill.: Crossway, 1991), 79.
30. See Strauch, *Biblical Eldership*, 67–83, for a thorough discussion of the qualifications of the elder.
31. Bennis, *Organizing Genius*, 197–98.
32. Osborne, *Unity Factor*, 42-45.
33. Ibid., 77–78; 92.
34. Ibid., 43–45.
35. Barna, *Habits of Highly Effective Churches*, 46–47.
36. Lynn Vincent, "Breaking Faith," *World Magazine* 17, no. 12 (30 March 2002), 20.
37. Consultation with the elders of Church of the Saviour, Wayne, Pennsylvania, January 28, 2002.
38. Gene Getz, *The Measure of a Man* (Glendale, Calif.: Regal, 1974); Alexander Strauch, *Biblical Eldership*; Paul Winslow and Dorman Followwill, *The Lord and the Elders* (Veradale, Wash.: Paul Winslow, 1999); Paul Winslow and Dorman Followwill, *Christ in Church Leadership: A Handbook for Elders and Pastors* (Grand Rapids: Discovery House, 2001).
39. John Carver and Miriam Mayhew Carver, *Basic Principles of Policy Governance* (San Francisco: Jossey-Bass, 1996).
40. Doyle and Straus, *How to Make Meetings Work,* 183–84.
41. Ibid., 183–85.
42. Barna, *Power of Team Leadership*, 24.
43. Robbins, *Organizational Behavior*, 260.
44. Barna, *Habits of Highly Effective Churches*, 54.
45. Ken Sande, *Managing Conflict in Your Church* (Billings, Mont.: Peacemaker Ministries, 1993), Appen. 2-8, nt.
46. Barna, *Habits of Highly Effective Churches*, 45.

NOTES

47. Strauch, *Meetings That Work: A Guide to Effective Elder Meetings* (Littleton, Co.: Lewis and Roth, 2001), 47.
48. John Piper, Sept. 24 to Dec. 10, 1995; www.desiringGOD.org.
49. Alliance for Non Profit Management, www.allianceonline.org; Strategic Planning, FAQ 7, 3.
50. Alliance for Non Profit Management, www.allianceonline.org; The Management Assistance Program for Nonprofits, www.mapfornonprofits.org.; Michael Allison and Jude Kaye, *Strategic Planning for Nonprofit Organizations: A Practical Guide and Workbook* (New York: Wiley, 1997).
51. Allison and Kaye, *Strategic Planning*, 1.
52. James Belasco and Jarve Stead, *Souring with the Phoenix* (New York: Warren, 1999), 239.
53. www.allianceonline.org; Strategic Planning, FAQ 7, 1.
54. Allison and Kaye, *Strategic Planning*, 68.
55. Ibid., 71.
56. Randy Pope, *The Prevailing Church: An Alternative Approach to Ministry* (Chicago: Moody, 2002), 93.
57. "Basics of Developing Mission, Vision, and Value Statements*,"* Management Assistance Program for Nonprofits; Library, Strategic Planning, www.mapfornonprofits.org.
58. Alliance for Nonprofit Management, Strategic Planning, FAQ 7, 3.
59. John F. Kennedy, Message to joint session of Congress, May 25, 1961.
60. James Kouzes and Barry Posner, *The Leadership Challenge: How to Keep Getting Extraordinary Things Done in Organizations* (San Francisco: Jossey-Bass, 1995), 106–07.
61. Barna, *Power of Team Leadership*, 24.
62. Christian Schwarz, *Natural Church Development: A Guide to Eight Essential Qualities of Healthy Churches*, (Carol Stream, Ill.: ChurchSmart Resources, 1996).
63. Ibid., 22–37.
64. Ibid.
65. George Barna, *Power of Vision* (Ventura, Calif.: Regal, 1997), 85.
66. Barna Research Group, Ltd., www.barna.org; The Gallup Organization, www.gallup.com.
67. Henry Mintzberg, *The Rise and Fall of Strategic Planning: Reconceiving Roles for Planning , Plans, Planners* (New York: Simon & Schuster, 1993).
68. Barna, *Power of Team Leadership*, 26.
69. Winslow and Followwill, *Christ in Church Leadership*, 127–35.
70. Private correspondence with author, February 19, 2002.
71. Edward Bratcher, *The Walk-On-Water Syndrome* (Waco, Tex.: Word, 1984), 22–35.
72. Brian Shilhavy, "Is the Pastorate Biblical? A Biblical Look at Leaders of the Church"; www.shilhavy.com/americanfamily, 2002.
73. Pope, *Prevailing Church*, 70–71.
74. Telephone conversation with author, March 9, 1995.

NOTES

75. Barna, *Power of Team Leadership*, 75.
76. Doyle and Straus, *How to Make Meetings Work*, 33–34.
77. Robert Nelson and Peter Economy, *Better Business Meetings* (New York: Irwin, 1995), 32.
78. Henry M. Robert, *The Scott Foresman Robert's Rules of Order Newly Revised* (New York: HarperCollins, 1990), xliv.
79. Doyle and Straus, *How to Make Meetings Work*, 75.
80. John Carver, *The Chairperson's Role as Servant-Leader to the Board* (San Francisco: Jossey-Bass, 1997), 1, 14.
81. Robert, *Robert's Rules*, Rule 42, 388–89.
82. Doyle and Straus, *How to Make Meetings Work,* 33.
83. Roger Fisher and William Ury, *Getting to Yes: Negotiating Agreement Without Giving In* (New York: Penguin, 1981), 41–57.
84. Ibid., 58–83.
85. Doyle and Straus, *How to Make Meetings Work,* 168.
86. Tom Peters and Robert Waterman, *In Search of Excellence: Lessons From America's Best Run Companies* (New York: Harper and Row, 1982).

BIBLIOGRAPHY

Alliance for Non Profit Management, www.allianceonline.org,

Allison, Michael and Jude Kaye. *Strategic Planning for Nonprofit Organizations: A Practical Guide and Workbook.* New York: Wiley, 1997.

Arndt, William F. and F. Wilber Gingrich (translated from Walter Bauer; revised and edited by Frederick W. Danker) *A Greek-English Lexicon of the New Testament and Other Early Christian Literature*, 3d ed. Chicago: University of Chicago, 2000.

Barna, George. *The Habits of Highly Effective Churches.* Ventura, Calif.: Regal Books, 1999.

——, *The Power of Vision.* Ventura, Calif.: Regal, 1997.

——, *The Power of Team Leadership.* Colorado Springs: WaterBrook, 2001.

"Basics of Developing Mission, Vision, and Value Statements," Management Assistance Program for Nonprofits, Library, Strategic Planning, www. mapfornonprofits.org.

Belasco, James, and Jarve Stead. *Souring with the Phoenix.* New York: Warren, 1999.

Bennis, Warren, and Patricia Ward Biederman. *Organizing Genius: The Secret of Creative Collaboration.* NewYork: Addison-Wesley, 1997.

Bratcher, Edward. *The Walk-On-Water Syndrome.* Waco, Tex.: Word, 1984.

Bruce, F. F. *The Book of the Acts.* Grand Rapids: Eerdmans, 1988.

Carver, John and Miriam Mayhew Carver. *Basic Principles of Policy Governance.* San Francisco: Jossey-Bass, 1996.

——. *The Chairperson's Role as Servant-Leader to the Board.* (San Francisco: Jossey-Bass, 1997.

Doyle, Michael, and David Straus. *How to Make Meetings Work.* New York: Jove, 1982.

BIBLIOGRAPHY

Fisher, Roger, and William Ury. *Getting to Yes: Negotiating Agreement Without Giving In.* New York: Penguin, 1981.

Getz, Gene. *The Measure of a Man.* Glendale, Calif.: Regal, 1974.

Kennedy, John F. Message to joint session of Congress. May 25, 1961.

Kittel, Gerhard, and Gerhard Friedrich. eds. *Theological Dictionary of the New Testament*, trans. Geoffrey W. Bromiley. Grand Rapids: Eerdmans, 1957.

Kouzes, James, and Barry Posner. *The Leadership Challenge: How to Keep Getting Extraordinary Things Done in Organizations.* San Francisco: Jossey-Bass, 1995.

Leadership Journal, www.LeadershipJournal.net, June 20, 2001.

The Management Assistance Program for Nonprofits, www.mapfornonprofits. org.

Mintzberg, Henry. *The Rise and Fall of Strategic Planning: Reconceiving Roles for Planning , Plans, Planners.* New York: Simon & Schuster, 1993.

Moreland, J. P. *Love Your God With All Your Mind: The Role of Reason in the Life of the Soul.* Colorado Springs: NavPress, 1997.

Nelson, Robert, and Peter Economy. *Better Business Meetings.* New York: Irwin, 1995.

Osborne, Larry. *The Unity Factor: Developing a Healthy Church Leadership Team.* Vista, Calif.: Owl's Nest, 2001.

Peters, Tom, and Robert Waterman. *In Search of Excellence: Lessons From America's Best Run Companies.* New York: Harper and Row, 1982.

Piper, John. Sept. 24 to Dec. 10, 1995. www.desiringGOD.org.

Piper, John, and Wayne Grudem. *Recovering Biblical Manhood and Womanhood: A Response to Evangelical Feminism.* Wheaton, Ill.: Crossway, 1991.

Pope, Randy. *The Prevailing Church: An Alternative Approach to Ministry.* Chicago: Moody, 2002.

Robbins, Stephen P. *Organizational Behavior*, 8th ed. Upper Saddle River, N.J.: Prentice Hall, 1997.

Robert, Henry M. *The Scott Foresman Robert's Rules of Order Newly Revised.* New York: HarperCollins, 1990.

Sande, Ken. *Managing Conflict in Your Church.* Billings, Mont.: Peacemaker Ministries, 1993.

Schwartz, Christian. *Natural Church Development: A Guide to Eight Essential Qualities of Healthy Churches.* Carol Stream, Ill.: ChurchSmart Resources, 1996.

BIBLIOGRAPHY

Shilhavy, Brian "Is the Pastorate Biblical? A Biblical Look at Leaders of the Church." www.shilhavy.com/americanfamily, 2002.

Strauch, Alexander. *Biblical Eldership: An Urgent Call to Restore Biblical Church Leadership* 3d ed. Littleton, Co.: Lewis and Roth, 1995.

——. *Meetings That Work: A Guide to Effective Elders' Meetings.* Littleton, Co.: Lewis and Roth, 2001.

——. *Ministry of Mercy: The New Testament Deacon.* Littleton, Co.: Lewis and Roth, 1992.

——. *The Study Guide to Biblical Eldership.* Littleton, Co.: Lewis and Roth, 1996.

Strauch, Alexander and Richard Swartley. *The Mentor's Guide to Biblical Eldership.* Littleton, Co.: Lewis and Roth, 1996.

Vincent, Lynn. "Breaking Faith," *World Magazine* 17, no. 12 (30 March 2002).

Wallace, David. "The Semantic Range of the Article-Noun-Kai-Noun Plural Construction in the New Testament," *Grace Theological Journal* 4 (Spring 1983).

Winslow, Paul and Dorman Followwill. *Christ in Church Leadership A Handbook for Elders and Pastors.* Grand Rapids: Discovery House, 2001.

——.*The Lord and the Elders.* Veradale, Wash.: Paul Winslow, 1999.

Scripture Index

Exodus
19:6   **17**

Deuteronomy
19:15   **156**

1 Samuel
8:4–7   **43**
8:5, 7   **28**

Psalms
133:1   **31, 125**

Matthew
16:19   **27**
16:23   **25**
18   **69–70**
18:15–16   **156**
18:15–18   **70**
18:17   **156**
18:18   **27**
18:19   **129**
23:1–2, 6–12   **27**
23:8, 10–12   **17**

Mark
3:14   **17**
6:7–13   **26**
10:35–45   **26**
10:42–45   **26**
10:43–44   **75**

John
5:19   **25**
5:30   **25**
10:12–13   **62**
13:1–15   **26**
13:8   **25**
13:34–35   **75**
14:10, 24   **25**

17:8   **25**
17:21   **31**
17:23   **125**

Acts
1:8   **96**
1:15–26   **30**
5:1–11   **28, 34**
6:1–6   **30**
6:4   **74**
10:1–48   **29**
11:1–18   **29**
11:27–30   **30**
13:1–3   **30**
13:3   **17**
14:23   **17, 19, 32, 50**
15   **17, 38, 62, 156**
15:1–22   **73**
15:1–35   **29**
15:4–25   **157–58**
15:7   **30**
15:22–23   **158**
15:36–41   **29**
15:39   **38**
15:40   **29**
16:1–3   **29**
16:4   **17**
16:4–5   **158**
20   **17, 89**
20:17, 28   **18**
20:20   **89**
20:28   **19, 37, 49, 56, 74–75**
20:28–31   **31, 67**
20:29–30   **34**
20:29–31   **126**
21:18   **17**

Romans
12:3–5; 6–7   **30**

12:4–8   **88**
12:10   **125**
14:10–11   **110**
15:14   **75**

1 Corinthians
1:10   **31, 125**
1:8–13   **30**
3:3   **31**
5:1–13   **29**
12:8–11; 28–31   **30**
12:14–30   **88**
12:27–30   **50**
12:29–30   **13**
14:8   **108**

Galatians
6:2   **75**

Ephesians
2:20   **28**
4:2   **125**
4:3   **125**
4:7–8   **75**
4:11   **13, 15–19, 88**
4:11–12   **50, 134**
4:11–13   **29**
4:12   **154**
4:12–13   **60**
4:12–16   **89**
5:1–2   **89**

Philippians
1:1   **18**
2:1–5   **125**
2:2   **31**
2:3–4   **75**

Colossians
1:18   **25, 37, 77**

SCRIPTURE INDEX

1:28   75
3:14   75, 125

1 Thessalonians
2:4–7   29
5:12   33, 38, 40, 52,
            76, 93, 99
5:12–13   20, 33, 50,
            73, 82, 98

1 Timothy
2:12   52 nt.
3   14, 50
3:1   56
3:1–7   74
3:1–13   16, 18
3:2   68
3:2–3   31, 140, 145
3:3   54
3:10   50
4:14   18 nt., 30
4:16   74

5:17   **14, 18, 20, 32**
5:18   33
5:19–21   68
5:22   51, 71

2 Timothy
2:2   50
2:24–25   31, 75

Titus
1   14, 50
1:5   11, 17, 19, 32, 50
1:5–9   16, 74
1:7   18
1:7, 9   160
1:7–8   54, 140
1:9   33, 38
1:9–11   34

Hebrews
13:17   20, 34, 51,
        73–74, 93, 98

James
5:14–15   30

1 Peter
2:9   17, 154
2:25   39
5:1   31, 62, 132
5:1–2   15, 18–19, 33
5:1, 5   73
5:2   56, 61, 74
5:4   39

2 John
1   62, 132

3 John
1   62, 132
8–9   31

General Index

A

abuse
  of power, **68-70**
  opposite-gender elationships, **70**
  private meeings, **70**
  proactive prevention, **70**
  restoration of the abuser, **71**
accountability, **121**
Acts 15, example, **157–58**
admonishment, **71**
advocate, **142–43**
agenda, **164–66**
Alliance for Non Profit Management, **102**, **107**
Allison, Michael, **107**
annual plan, **104**, **117–20**
apostles
  authority, **28, 62, 132**
  intent for the church, **19–21, 22–23**
  role, **13–14, 33**
  teaching, **28**
apostolic delegates, **13–14**
appeals
  committee decisions, **92**
  discipline decisions, **71–72**
archō, **20**
Armstrong, John H., **71** nt.
authority
  administrative, **73**
  apostolic, **28, 62, 132**
  elder, **37, 72**
  exercised primarily through teaching, **34**
  exercising, **71–72**
  individual, **27, 62, 79**
  not like Gentile rulers, **26**
  not over other disciples, **26**
  not over other elders, **20**
  of pastor, **47**
  women, **52**

B

bad decisions
  natural causes, **151–52**
  spiritual causes, **152–53**
Barna, George, **35, 36, 40, 47, 59, 84, 89, 93, 113, 116, 134**
barriers to consensus
  bias, **139**
  inadequate preparation, **137–38**
  inappropriate use of *Robet's Rules of Order*, **138**
  micromanagement, **136–37**
  short-term memory, **139–40**
Belasco, James, **103**
Bennis, Warren, **32, 35**
Bethlehem Baptist Church, **97, 132–33**
bias, **139**
biblical character,
  loss of, **8, 25, 94**
Biblical Eldership, **8, 13, 37, 160**
biblical governance,
  prerequisites, **73–75**
bicameral government, **86**
binding and loosing, **27**
bivocational, **33, 46–47, 57, 61, 86, 94, 168**. *See* tentmakers.
board of directors, **20, 37, 40, 58, 77–78, 84, 87**
board of trustees, **91**
brainstorm, **110, 150**
Bratcher, Edward B., **131**
Bruce, F. F., **29** nt.
bylaws, **25, 52, 72–73, 138, 148**

C

calling
  elder, **50–51, 54–58, 61**
  missionaries, **56–57**
  preacher, **56–57**
Can Fallen Pastors Be Restored?, **71**
  nt.
Carver, John, **77–78, 141**
Carver, Miriam Mayhew, **77**
CarverGuide, **141**
chairman, **124, 135–141, 147–48**
cheirotoneō, **17**
church
  biblical, **21, 23, 78–79**
  Christ as head, **20**
  governed by a plurality of elders,
      **19, 21, 24, 28, 32, 34–37, 80–
      81, 88, 125–26**
  large, **44**
  New Testaent, **12–13, 32–34, 42,
      47–48, 81–84, 93–96, 157–58**
  singular Head, **28**
  small, **12–13, 25, 44, 47, 80–81,
      89**
church growth movement, **24**
Church of the Saviour, **9, 44–45**
church planters, **14, 27, 33**
church plants, **44, 82–83**
ChurchSmart Resources, **113**
clergy, **16 nt., 76, 93**
collaboration, **35**
commissioning, **30, 53**
commissions, **79, 85, 89, 92.** *See*
  teams
committees, **79, 87, 91–92**
communication
  congregations obligations, **98–99**
  distributed approach, **97–98**
  venues, **96–97**
confidentiality, **91, 156, 158–60**
consensus
  defined, **128–29**
  facilitating, **149–50**
  functional barriers, **136–40**
  threats to, **129–36**
core beliefs, **106**
council
  communication, **163–64**
  proactive leadership, **79–80**
council decisions
  avocate of proposal, **142–43**
  bad decisions, **151–53**
  closed session, **155–56, 159**
  congregational involvement, **154**
  disseminating, **154**
  elders and staff bound by, **73**
  facilitating consensus, **149–50**
  facilitator, **146–48**
  handling an impasse, **150–51**
  introducing the topic, **143**
  New Testament precedent, **154–
      55**
  preparing the council, **144–45**
  preparing the proposal, **143–44**
  presentation to the council, **145–
      46**
council meetings
  agenda, **164–66**
  complaints about, **123–24**
  ministry reports, **167–68**
  minutes, **168–69**
  prayer, **167**
  virtual, **166–67**
covenant, **71–72**

D

deacons
  office, **14**
  responsibilities, **14**
decisions
  consensus, **128–29**
  emergency, **160–61**
  handling major, **142–53**
  majority vote, **127**
  unanimous consent, **125–27**
  unity defined, **125**
  unity urged, **125**
delegation
  according to gifting, **88–89**
  enhances oversight, **92–93**
  method, **85**
  necessity for, **88–92**
didaskalos, **15**
disciples were equals, **26**
discipline
  of abuser, **71**
  administered by commision or
      committee, **91**
  church, **71–72**
diversity of gifts, **46, 88–89**
double honor, **32–33**
Doyle, Michael, **39, 84, 138, 147,
  151**

GENERAL INDEX

E

Economy, Peter, **137**
elder appointment
  by the Holy Spirit, **49–50, 54–57,
    77, 81, 87**
  council's role, **54–55**
  lack of candidates, **55–56**
  limitations on the role of the
    congregation, **50–52**
  necessary role of congregation,
    52–54
  New Testament background, **50**
elder board, **11–12, 37, 40, 123**
elder council
  delegation to a smaller team, **85–
    88**
  not a board of directors, **78**
  practical size limit, **83**
  relationship with congregation, **96**
  role, **54–55**
  rotating members, **64–65**
  size, **80–84**
  size dilemma, **83–84**
  size in large churches, **81–82**
  size in smaller churches, **80–81**
  teaching as chief avenue of
    leadership, **96**
elder emeritus, **65–66**
elder governance, distortion of, **38–
  41**
elder recruitment, inadequate
  solutions, **61**
elders
  accountability, **67**
  appointment of, **49**
  calling, **56–58**
  corporate responsibilities, **77**
  divison of labor, **15**
  exercising authority, **71–73**
  leading, **20**
  mandatory rotation, **63**
  moral authority, **71**
  office of, **14**
  plurality, **19, 32–35, 37, 81, 133**
  ruling, **14**
  specialization, **14**
  term limits, **63**
  wives of, **159**
elite group, **80**
email, **144, 163–66**
entry-level opportunities, **60**

environment
  changing, **103**
  church, **47**
  conducive to leadership
    development, **59–61**
  diferent from early church, **24**
  external, **112**
  internal, **112**
episkopeō, **18**
evangelists, **13, 15, 33, 50, 63**

F

facilitator, **146–51**
fellow elder, **62**
financial administration
  delgation, **91**
  subordinate to council, **91–92**
first among equals, **42–43**
Fisher, Roger, **149**
Followwill, Dorman, **76, 127**

G

gatekeeper, **59**
Getting to Yes, **149**
gifts, **13, 15–16**
goals, **116–17**
Goins, Doug, **127, 134**
governance, biblical principles, **37–
  38**
Grace Fellowship Church, **44**
Great Commission, **11, 100**
Great Group, **35**
groups cannot lead, **88**
groupthink, avoiding, **151–52**
Grudem, Wayne, **52** nt.

H

handling an impasse, **150–51**
historical perspective, **80**
house fellowships, **19**
How to Make Meetings Work, **39**

I

*If Ministers Fall, Can They Be
  Restored?*, **71** nt.
immature men, **64**
impasse, **150-51**

GENERAL INDEX

In Search of Excellence, **171**
inadequate preparation, **137–38**
introducing the topic, **143**

J

Janis, Irving L., **151**
Jerusalem council, **17, 29, 62, 157–58**

K

Kaye, Jude, **107**
kathistēmi, **17**
Kennedy, President John F., **109**
Kouzes, James, **110**

L

LaHaye, Tim, **71** nt.
lawsuits, **72, 153**
leaders
    strained relation with wife, **70**
    unmarried, **70**
leadership
    apostle's teaching on, **28–32**
    by corporate board, **40**
    by oligarchy, **39, 85, 136**
    by passive board, **40, 84**
    by pseudo team, **41**
    collective, **9, 19, 26–38, 44, 76–80, 101**
    democratic, **39**
    four essential approaches, **35–36**
    Jesus' teaching on, **26–28**
    not abrogated by collective responsibility, **32**
leadership team
    communcation with council, **86**
    degree of delegated responsibility, **87**
    frequency of meetings, **87**
    members permanent, **86**
    multiple leaders, **88**
    non-members share in governing authority, **85**
    not a separate legislative body, **86**
legal exposure, **72**
Littleton Bible Chapel, **44**
Lone Ranger, **35**

M

MacNamara, Carter, **107**
major decisions
    definition, **142**
    preparing the council, **144–45**
    preparing the proposal, **143–44**
    presentation to the council, **144–45**
managers, passive, **78**
meetings
    closed, **155–59**
    face-to-face, **166**
    open, **155–56**
meetings, closed, alternatives to, **155–57**
megachurch, **24**
member covenant, **71–72**
membership, **72, 99**
Mentor's Guide to Biblical Eldership, **55** nt., **160** nt.
micromanagement, **136–37**
ministry assistants, **94**
ministry reports, **167–68**
Mintzberg, Henry, **116** nt.
minutes, **86, 91, 158–59, 163–64, 168–69**
mission statement, **111**
moderator
    limits on authority, **72–73**
    role, **140–41, 145–48**
    title, **141**
    training, **65**
Moreland, J. P., **22** nt., **35**

N

Natural Church Development, **112**
Nelson, Robert, **137**
new blood, **64**
New Testament Churches,
    governed by elders, **32–34**
nondisclosure, **158–60**
nonprofit corporation, **77**

O

objectives, **117**
oligarchy, **39, 85, 136**
on-the-job training, **59**
opposite-gender relationships, **70**

GENERAL INDEX

ordaining, **17**
organizational structures, **23**
organizations
    for profit, **77**
    hierarchial, **38**
    horizontal, **38**
    non-profit, **77**
    owners, **77–78**
Organizing Genius, **35**
Osborne, Larry, **12–13**
oversee, **18**
overseer, not a separate office, **18**
oversight, enhanced by delegation,
    92–93

P

pastor
    as position title, **61–62**
    derivation of title, **14–16**
    not a position, **16**
    not a separate office, **16–19**
pastor-teacher, **15**
Peacemaker Ministries, **72 nt., 92**
peer relationships, **81, 132**
peer reviews, **67–68**
peithō, **20, 34**
Peninsula Bible Churches, **9, 44, 127,
    134**
Perimeter Church, **107**
Peters, Tom, **171**
Piper, John, **52 nt., 97, 131–32**
planning
    caution, **121–22**
    cycle, **121**
    necessity of, **100**
plurality, **19, 32–35, 37, 81, 133**
poieō, **17**
poimēn, **15–16**
policy manual, **169–70**
Pope, Randy, **107, 133**
Posner, Barry, **110**
power imbalance, **69–70**
Power of Team Leadership, **35–36**
prayer
    elder, **167**
    lack of, **123, 130–31, 153**
preachers, **23, 27, 32, 41, 46, 56–57,
    62, 131–35**
presbyterion, **18**. *See* elder council.
presbyteros. **18**. *See* elder.
presbytery, **18** nt.

Prevailing Church, **133**
proïstēmi, **20, 101**
prophets, **13, 15, 28, 50**
purpose statement, **111**

R

rebellion, **73**
reporting, **121**
Reverend, title, **17**
Rise and Fall of Strategic Planning,
    116 nt.
Robbins, Stephen, **32, 43, 85**
Robert's Rules
    dilemma, **148**
Robert's Rules of Order, **138, 147,
    148**
role of the preacher, **131–35**
rotation
    disruptive, **64**
    leads to staff dominance, **64**
    officers, **65**
rule, unitary, **28**
Russell, Dr. Walt, **9**

S

Sande, Ken, **91–92**
Schaller, Lyle, **133**
Schwarz, Christian, **112**
secrecy, **158**
seminary graduate, **33**
senior pastor
    assessment of role, **39–40, 45–46**
    model, **131–35**
sexual abuse, **69**
shared goals, **101**
shared leadership, **42, 74**
shared pulpit
    care in implementation, **45–46**
    discription, **44–45**
shared values, **106**
shepherds, **16, 33, 50**
Shilhavy, Brian, **33, 132**
short-term memory, **139–40**
small group, **60**
Soaring With the Phoenix, **103**
staff
    background checks, **96**
    divided loyalty, **62**
    hiring from outside, **94–96**
    hiring from within, **94**

inhibits team effort, **41**
integration with volunteers, **94**
meets apart from elders, **79**
over dependance on, **58–59**
reference checks, **95**
relationship to elder council, **93**
Stead, Jarve, **103**
strategic planning
  elements, **104**
  goals, **117**
  mission statement, **111**
  objectives, **117**
  process, **105**
  purpose statement, **101**
  shared values, **106**
  strategies, **115–16**
  SWOT Analysis, **113–15**
  tactics, **118**
  terminology, **102–3**
  top-down planning, **101**
  vision statement, **107**
strategies, **115–16**
Strauch, Alexander, **8, 13–14, 37, 55**
  nt., **76, 97, 160**
Straus, David, **39, 84, 138, 147, 151**
Study Guide to Biblical Eldership, **55**
  nt., **160**
successful implementations, **44**
Support Center for Nonprofit
  Management, **107**
Swartley, Richard, **55** nt., **160** nt.
SWOT analysis
  definition, **112**
  example, **114**

T

tactics, **118**
teachers, **13, 17, 44**
teaching, chief avenue of elder's
  leadership, **96**
team ministry, **94, 121, 134–35,**
teams, **41, 43, 46–47, 55, 58, 85–94.**
  See commissions.

teamwork in the pulpit, **44–46**
tentmakers
  definition, **33, 60, 94**
  equal partners with staff elders,
    46–47
threats to consensus
  domination by one or a few, **135–
    36**
  lack of prayer, **130–31**
  role of the preacher, **131–35**
titles, **27**
top-down planning, **101**

U

unity
  not always possible, **32**
  urged, **32**
Unity Factor, **12**
unmarried leaders, dating, **70**
unqualified elder, removal, **65**
Ury, William, **149**

V

virtual meetings, **166–67**
vision
  creating, **108**
  definition, **107**
  statement characteristics, **108–9**
  stimulating creation process, **110–
    11**
vocational elders, **56, 60–61, 87**
volunteers, **48, 58, 82, 93–94**

W

wages, **33**
Walk-On-Water Syndrome, **131**
Waterman, Robert, **171**
Web pages, **97, 163–64**
Winslow, Paul, **76, 127**

About the Author

RICHARD SWARTLEY is a retired advanced space systems manager and senior systems engineer from Lockheed Martin. He has a Masters in Divinity and is a founding elder of Church of the Saviour in Wayne, Pennsylvania, a nondenominational church founded in 1972, presently with an adult attendance of two thousand. In the past, Dick served two terms as the chairman of the church's elders. In the mid-nineties, he was instrumental in the restructuring of the church from a senior pastor framework to team ministry, with three elders sharing the pulpit. He is active as an elder, author, church consultant, and counselor.

Other books by Richard Swartley include:

> *The Mentor's Guide to Biblical Eldership: Twelve Lessons for Mentoring Men for Eldership*
> (coauthored with Alexander Strauch)

> *The Right Start Premarital Program Sexual Attitudes and Understanding Test*

Books coauthored with Anne Swartley:

> *The Right Start Premarital Program Student Notebook*
> *The Right Start Premarital Program Student Workbook*
> *The Right Start Premarital Program Mentors' Guide*
> *The Right Start Premarital Program Coordinators' Manual*
> *Communication Workbook for Married Couples*
> *Communication Workbook for Married Couples Facilitators' Guide*

Richard Swartley can be contacted at richardswartley@aol.com

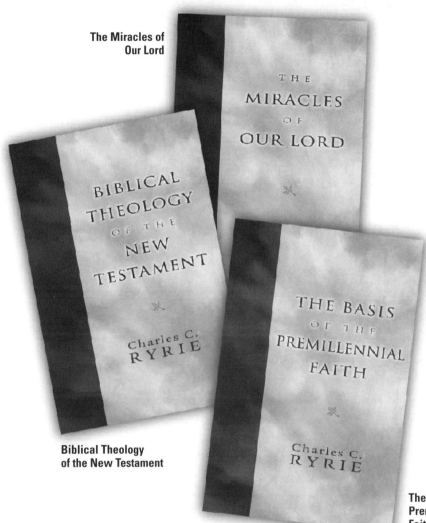